# Lost the Plot

## PART ONE

## Half Plot

## Publisher

ISBN: 978-0-9575812-0-3

Published by: Allotment Junkie

Design: Twistedgifted ©

Set in:

Helvetica, LloydsHand, Impact, Sketch Rockwell, Marker Felt, Webdings, Zapf Dingbats

Printed and bound by: Butler Tanner and Dennis

GREAT BRITISH BOOKS™ PUBLISHED & PRINTED IN THE UK

**FSC**
www.fsc.org

**MIX**
Paper from responsible sources
FSC® C023561

Are you an
# allotment
# JUNKIE
## Bookworm

**LOOK WHAT'S COOKING...**

Other books in the series coming soon.

Visit: www.allotmentjunkie.com

All diggin', weeding, building, sowing, planting, watering, harvesting, eating, sleeping, writing, designing, graphics, photography, spell-checking, proofreading, artwork and children – produced by: Paul King and Claire Lakey.

# MENU

## Welcome to our Plot

**Ingredients:**
10% Imagination, 90% Perspiration

Contains no artificial colours or flavours. Store in a garden shed; read for inspiration. Suitable for vegetarians ▽

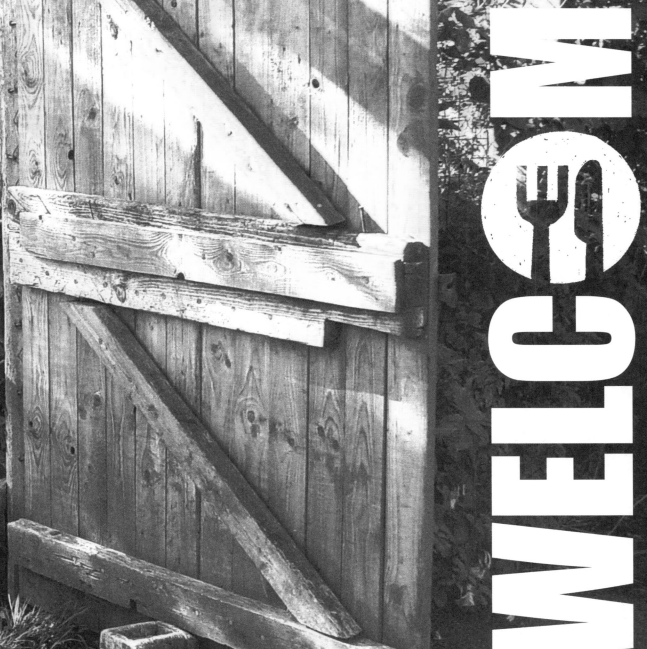

WELCOME

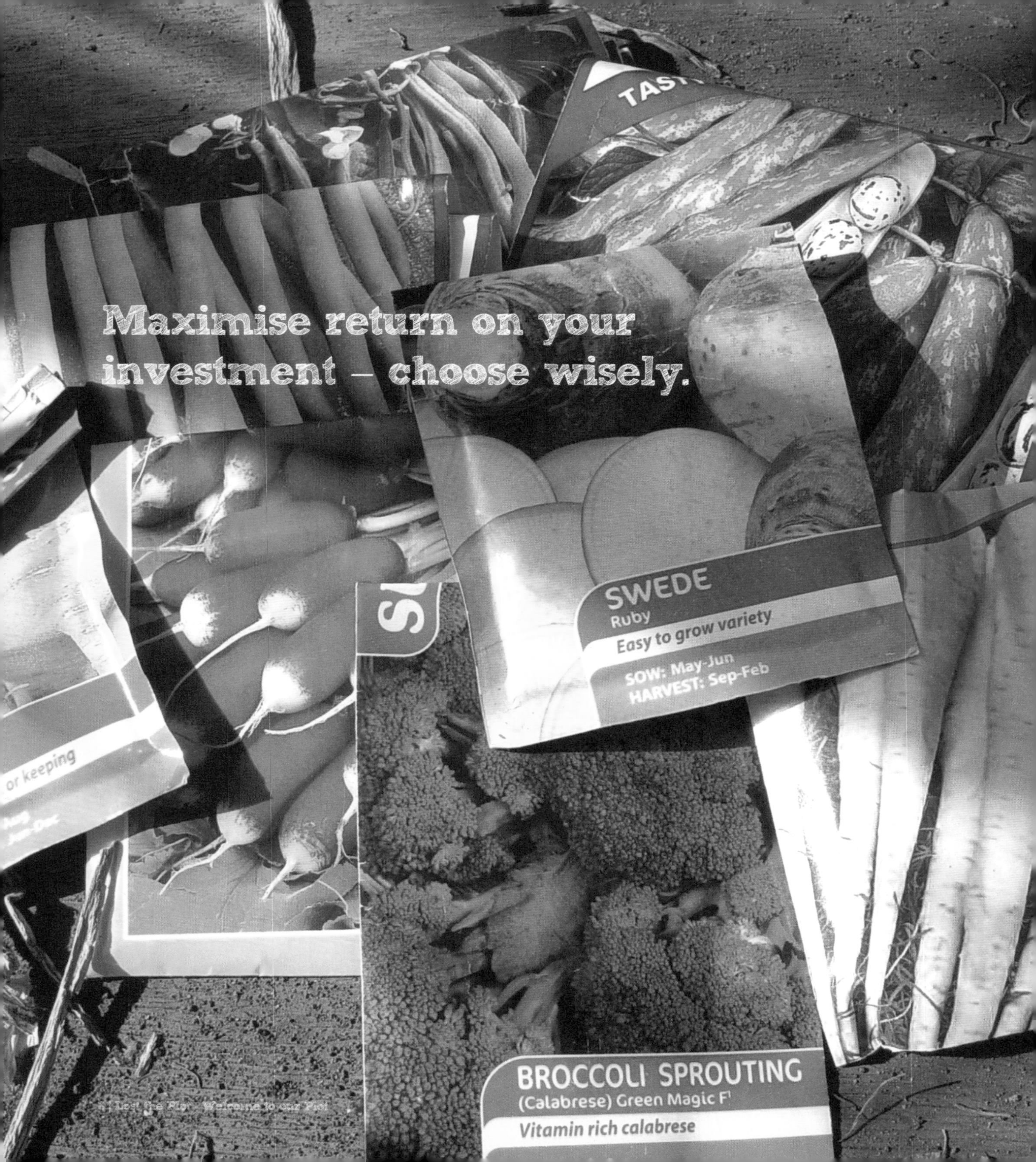

Maximise return on your investment – choose wisely.
TAST
SWEDE
Ruby
Easy to grow variety
SOW: May-Jun
HARVEST: Sep-Feb
or keeping
BROCCOLI SPROUTING
(Calabrese) Green Magic F1
Vitamin rich calabrese

# Lost the Plot

**I'm now a self-confessed Allotment Junkie, and three years on – still learning and loving it! Looking back to how it all started, I can't help but wonder why Claire and I decided to take on a lost plot. It was not the logical garden path for us as a couple; we are both from creative backgrounds, with little or no experience in horticulture, gardening – or growing veg for that matter.**

It all started when Maya Sahara, our eldest daughter, was born. That year also gave birth to the romantic notion of growing our own fresh organic veg, hoping to give Maya her '5-a-day' and the very best of starts.

Claire has been a vegetarian for 28 years, so the thought of home-grown organics really appealed to her. And so she agreed to muck in – even though she is more of a city chick than a farmer's wife! For my own part, growing our own veg, especially in times of recession, was just another way of contributing to the family table.

Thinking we could sign up, pay the fees and start growing there and then, it was a real surprise to find a waiting list instead, to which our names were duly added. So we took on our plot in 2008 (Season One) while juggling our time as new parents and running a small design agency. Since those early days, the plot has become more important than we ever imagined. As the downturn began to bite, I became more and more cash-poor and time-rich, so keeping busy on the plot with its solitude and fresh air ensured that I didn't 'lose the plot'.

More importantly, over the past few seasons, growing our own has turned from pastime to passion, which we hope to share with you.

## Meet the team

**Paul, Claire and Maya.** Part of the reason for taking on an allotment was to teach Maya about growing fruit and vegetables. Educating her about food, where it comes from and all the different varieties we could grow, as well as getting outdoors more, learning about the seasons and seeing the local wildlife.

I say we took on the allotment partly to teach Maya how to grow fruit and veg, but it was a real learning curve for us all. Having not really grown anything before, we were no authority on the subject ourselves. Traditionally, grandparents in the family would pass on these skills; however, ours have never shown any real interest in gardening but remember the days of 'Dig for Victory' and 'Make Do and Mend'. Having taken on the plot, where to start was the big question for us, having now realised what we had got ourselves into. The only real concept we had was to grow our veggies organically. But even as I write this, the word organic is an ideology – a word used in the local deli. I didn't appreciate or understand what this really entailed or how to achieve it, let alone try to teach Maya. Fortunately, Claire is a vegetarian of 28 years, and a home cook, so the temptation of fresh organics really had her sold. It's mainly due to her enthusiasm for fresh deliciously tasting ingredients that inspired my effort on the kitchen garden and this book.

**Success at last!** It has only taken three seasons to finally achieve a crop of carrots – and all with the help of Maya.

**Season One:** Followed the instructions on the packet. Carrot fly and slugs got the crop.

**Season Two:** Companion planting. Very poor results. Slugs got the crop.

**Season Three:** Belts and braces approach – raised bed and micro-netting with beer traps for the slugs. **Result!**

Children like to see things happen quickly and these little beauties are possibly the easiest veggies in the garden to grow.

# stuffed

## courgette flowers – a culinary revelation

## Self-sufficiency

Having taken on your allotment, and depending on the time of year, you may achieve a first crop – but the name of the game is patience. Clearing and cultivating a half plot can take anything up to a year – assuming that you can give one day on a weekend and at least a couple of evenings in the summer months. Becoming self-sufficient in fruit and veg is a goal that the whole family must be enthusiastic about in order to achieve. It's a long-term investment and can initially be an expensive hobby. The reasons for taking on an allotment will differ between people but, with inflation at an all-time high and the rising cost of fresh fruit and veg, an allotment can become a real asset to today's family. One key factor that remains the same for all of us is *time* – the hours we spend on site as well as the passing of the seasons. Because most of us are not full-time gardeners, juggling our time between work and family commitments and the fact it takes several seasons to learn the skills required – from trial and error as well as tuition from the wise on the allotment – time management is the key here to your success.

When we talk about being self-sufficient at this early stage, we mean 'summer' self-sufficient, being able to grow fruit and veg over a six-to-nine-month period. Being able to produce fruit and veg 'all year round' from your allotment is not an impossibility – but the very fact that we live in a country where even the summers are poor weather-wise, can make this very difficult to achieve even for the well-established growers with decades of experience. The aim is to achieve a bountiful crop and harvest from as early in the year as possible and learn how to extend your growing season as far as possible into the winter and on into the following year.

## Over-subscription

With the surge of interest in growing your own fruit and veg over the past few years, there is now a real shortage of available plots on council-run allotments – demand now outstrips supply. Most allotments have long waiting lists and many committees now divide full plots into two. Even a half plot of 70 x 15ft can seem a daunting task, especially if the plot you are taking on has been unkept for a few years and overgrown with 10ft-tall bramble bushes.

Part of the reason for putting this book together was to help you keep focused with ideas and progress to a productive veg patch. Bear in mind that some people, maybe you, have had to wait two years to get a plot.

**Where to look for help finding an allotment**
If you have internet access, searching 'find an allotment' could be a good first step. You could also look on your local authority's website and search for 'allotments', or under 'leisure/outdoors', and navigate to 'parks and open spaces'. They may have an online database of available sites and waiting lists. You need the name and contact details of the allotment manager and apply directly. Also visit these two sites as a good source of interest on the topic:

www.nsalg.org.uk  www.landshare.net

## Plan ahead

**When you are lucky enough to be handed the keys to the allotment gates and have your own plot, it may be worthwhile, with the help of this book, to plan ahead.**

You would have chosen your plot from those available – hopefully the one next to the water supply rather than the one with the least amount of work to do. **Take time to measure the plot, plan and design the layout (see page 30) on graph paper, and do it to scale (see page 152). This is how the professionals do it.**

Set timescales, achievable goals season by season. If you are really keen, learn about the different methods of cultivating the land: no-dig, straight rows or raised beds – all of which have their advantages and disadvantages. There are many wonderful books available that explain all these systems in detail – from The Victorian Kitchen Garden to the Shakers philosophy and the tools they made.

Our first mistake was to clear the entire site and trench-dig front to back. This was back-breaking work and, with hindsight, needn't have been. When all your weekends are given over to working the land and weeding, it's a sure fire way to lose interest very quickly.

**Some key things to remember:**

- Paths need to be about 2ft wide – it's not a written law but helps when navigating a wheelbarrow around the site.
- Plan for a compost bin or composting area, and I don't mean a black Dalek! 1000sqft of allotment can produce a lot of material. Don't put it behind the shed as it can get smelly when the sun is out – unpleasant if having that barbecue with your friends!
- If you go with a raised bed system, design the layout so you can reach the middle of the bed from the paths that surround it, so that you don't have to walk on the soil in the actual bed. Remember, you'll also need to fill them will soil or compost – so don't build them 3ft high unless you have the material.
- Don't forget a relaxation area; most people have it next to the shed with a bench or a few chairs to put your feet up with a cuppa – well away from the compost bin!

Plan for a shed, but don't rush out to buy it straight away – unless you know you are really very keen.

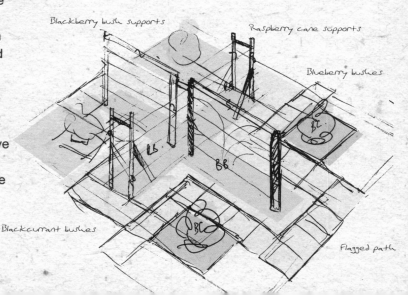

These architectural climbing beans will add a sense of perspective to the overall design layout of your plot with their height. Many veg growers take great pride in the aesthetics of their plots as well as the delivery of a bountiful harvest.

Try to get the plot next to the water supply and plan to get water butts in place as soon as possible. In 2010, some places in the UK had a hosepipe ban for at least eight weeks.

Lost the Plot

# Tools of the trade

Depending on what you want to achieve with your allotment – growing veg, flowers or just laying that perfect green lawn – you will need some of the following tools:

## GARDENING TOOLS and KIT

1. Wheelbarrow
2. Garden canes
3. Digging spade
4. Dutch hoe
5. Digging fork
6. Children's spade (if you have kids!)
7. Garden rake
8. Cultivator
9. Pricker, dibber and labels
10. Twine or string
11. Atomiser and spray gun
12. Hand fork/trowel and root-weeder
13. Children's gloves (if you have kids!)
14. Incinerator
15. Barbecue
16. Scissors, bottle-opener and secateurs
17. Steel toe boots

A. Pushbike
B. Tea/soup flask
C. Hayfever/allergy tablets or drops

## DIY TOOLS

1. 3 – 6" nails and screws
2. Heavy-duty DIY gloves
3. Cordless drill
4. Tape measure
5. Saw
6. Crosshead screwdriver
7. Flathead screwdriver
8. Spirit level
9. Safety glasses
10. Lump hammer
11. Brick bolster
12. Sharp knife
13. Selection of spanners
14. Wood drill bit
15. Pencil

## OTHER USEFUL TOOLS

Brush hook, bypass loppers pruning saw, hedge shears

The four tools listed (but not pictured) above would be a real advantage if your plot is overgrown, wild and out of order.

**Become a real eco warrior – get on your bike!**

Allotment sites are usually within a ten-minute walk from where you live, so there's no excuse – leave the car at home. Dust down the bike that's been in the shed going nowhere, put a basket on the front or get a trailer to achieve a zero carbon footprint to and from your plot. If you have kids, get them out on bikes too! If you're working, you could even get a new tax-free bike through the Cycle to Work scheme, which for most people means you will save around 40% of the cost. Visit **www.cyclescheme.co.uk** for more information.

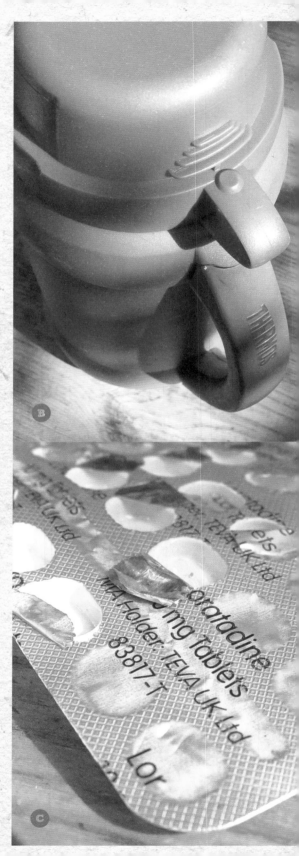

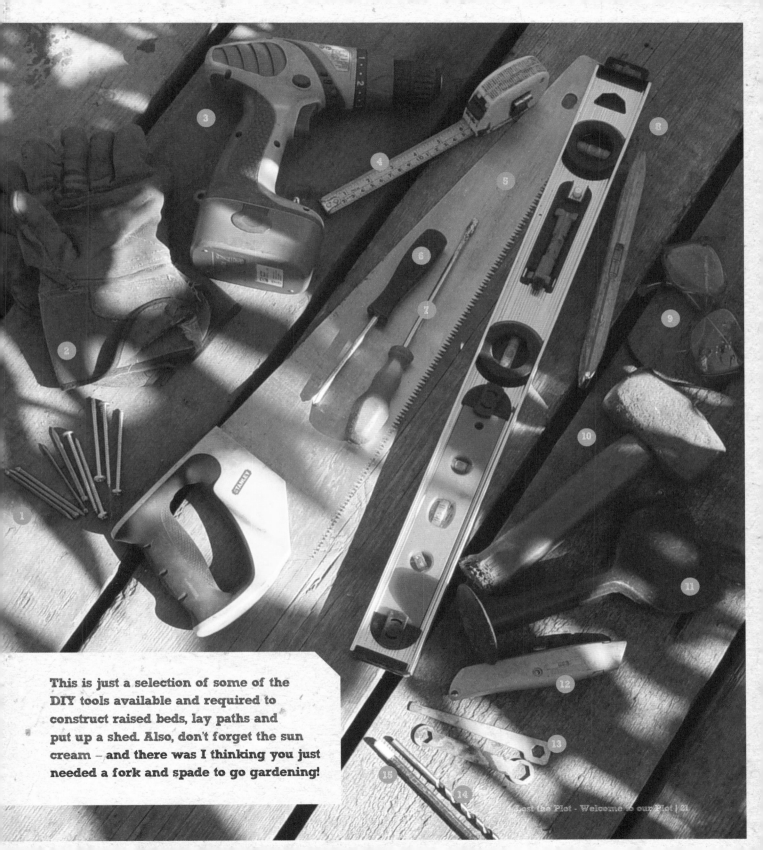

This is just a selection of some of the DIY tools available and required to construct raised beds, lay paths and put up a shed. Also, don't forget the sun cream – and there was I thinking you just needed a fork and spade to go gardening!

Courgettes are a super-easy firecracker of a veg to grow – great for kids. Chillies are far trickier – they need up to 30 days at a controlled temperature in order to germinate. Mushrooms need more than muck and a dark room, contrary to what people may say!

## Planning what to grow

The choice of seed is vast and can be costly, so choose wisely. Garden centres have a very good choice and are usually the first port of call for many, but it's worth noting that a few packets can soon add up, so be careful not to get carried away. Don't forget you'll also need the tools for the job in hand. There are specialist seed suppliers who produce catalogues with full colour photographs, which they will post out free of charge. You can then make a list of what you need and it's easier to stay in control of your spending too. Also, they have websites that work. Many of the old-timers still prefer to send off cheques with their orders, but the internet is now just another tool for the modern veg grower. The excitement of what to sow and grow is something to get the whole family involved in. At this stage, choose hardy veg and quick salads, depending on the time of year. Also, bear in mind the amount of hard work still involved in clearing your plot and cultivating the land ready to grow edible food (flick over the next few chapters to see what you could potentially face). Look for crops that are not too difficult to grow or that are too needy. With them, you'll be more likely to be rewarded in abundance, giving you your first taste of success and spurring you on to further cultivate your plot as well as your knowledge.

**If you have taken your plot on in the spring**
Onion sets, potatoes, sweetcorn, broad beans, salad leaves, beetroots, courgettes and sunflowers will get you off to a good start.

**If you have taken the plot on in the autumn**
Hardy overwinter onion sets, garlic and spring cabbage. Fruiting trees, plants and bushes can be planted now – give thought to what they need to flourish when planning the layout of your garden and give them space. They are long-term investments that will reward in abundance if you get it right when planting out.

Tomato Money Maker and Gardener's Delight are a popular choice. Why not try Golden Sunrise, which is bright yellow and not often seen in the supermarket? It looks and tastes delicious in a salad. The choice is wonderful; beef, plum, cherry – you'll soon need that full plot!

Keep a lookout for seed packets given away monthly with gardening magazines, such as Grow Your Own or Grow it! They're also packed with tips too and a pleasure to flick through during your breaks on the plot.

Filled with crumbly ricotta and soft goat's cheese dipped in batter and deep-fried. It's a taste sensation and revelation in our home kitchen. (thanks Jamie)

## Vandalism

It's worth commenting on vandalism as it will inevitably affect you, either directly or indirectly, once you are in the allotment community. Most allotments are local council-run sites: you pay a fee (currently £27.50 per year per half plot in our case) to rent the land for the purpose of growing your own veg. However, nearly all these sites are reclaimed or wasteland pushed to one side on the outskirts of town or city. Our allotment, in south Manchester, has an 8ft-high steel security fence surrounding it, which is smeared with anti-climb paint to the very top spikes, and CCTV cameras to cover the main gate.

You may question the romance of growing your own fruit and veg the first time you arrive on site – as we did, especially when little people are involved. But don't be alarmed. The odd spade may go missing or the polytunnel may get slashed, but allotmenteering, as you will learn, is about being resourceful – use a little common sense and bend to whatever nature or a few misguided individuals can throw at you.

## Safety first

The 'peaceful' pastime of gardening accounts for a huge amount of injuries seen in Accident and Emergency units each year. For most, the odd brush with a nettle plant is quick to remedy. However, a garden cane in the eye is a different story – so pay due care and diligence at all times, especially if you're not so hands-on with DIY tools and plan on building raised beds or putting up a shed. Even some of the basic gardening tools are reminiscent of medieval weaponry – so care is required. If children are going to be on site, spend time beforehand to clear up after previous tenants. Make sure all water storages are securely covered, tools are tidy and not lying around. Any chemicals, used or leftover, should be out of reach or discarded of in the correct fashion away from the plot.

**Remember, children don't see danger.**

The weather is another factor that must be considered: sunburn and dehydration in the summer months, as well as the risk of slipping or falling on frost or ice in the winter months. Most people today have mobile phones, but if you don't have one yet, now may be a good time to invest in one. Sometimes an allotment site can be a quiet place with no one to be seen all day long, so it's good to know help is a call away – just in case.

**Part One:** Taking on a plot is not an instructional manual on how to grow fruit and veg. It's a book of inspiration, we hope. It's hard work with mixed results at times, but with plenty to learn – from the science of soil culture, the many pests and diseases, to learning how to grow the veggies in the first place – it can be a fun and rewarding activity within a friendly, family-orientated community.

 **If we, as a family, can do it, so can you!**

## Comments from Claire

My main reason for taking on an allotment differs slightly from that of my 'partner in grime', Paul. Yes, I loved the idea of having an abundant supply of fresh, deliciously tasting seasonal vegetables; being a vegetarian for close to thirty years, they are my staple food after all. I would even go so far as to agree with the 'getting exercise' and 'fresh air' element of the venture.

But the real reason I wanted to do this came after watching a celebrity chef show on TV. He was asking British children what the various vegetables he was holding up were. I was horrified to note they couldn't even recognise the humble spud. I bet they know what a chip looks like, yet not from where it comes!

At the opposite end of the spectrum, the Italian children knew every single vegetable he showed them. Maya was just a baby at the time and I instantly thought, "No child of mine is going to grow up not knowing where their food comes from."

I am pleased to report that Maya most definitely knows her vegetables and understands exactly where they come from!

**Now the hard work begins...** Lost the Plot

# Lost the Plot

## Year 1

### Start Here

Jungle Warfare

# Has anyone seen my trowel?

Only after advice from the wise on the allotment did I decide not to hire a mini-digger and rotavator for a week. Any perennial weeds such as couch grass, docks, nettles and bindweed meticulously had to be taken out by hand for fear of them getting chopped up, spreading and multiplying.

## It's just not funny.

# Jungle Warfare

**This is just the tip of the iceberg. It's what lies below the surface that is the real problem. So how do you turn an overgrown patch like this into a productive veg bed?**

·········· HARD WORK ··········

This is a real-life insight into what is involved with stewardship of an allotment. Over the course of this book we break it down task by task, season by season.

You'll be surprised how quickly the top vegetation can be cut down to ground level, revealing how the previous tenant cultivated the plot. In our case, it looks like a no-dig system was operated for many years, so we had to learn the art of jungle warfare and weed assassination.

Taking on an unkept plot

- Have a pair of heavy-duty gardening or DIY gloves to hand, even safety glasses and boots
- Cover your arms and don't wear shorts. Brambles are vicious, have no respect and painfully tear the unprotected skin
- Take a packed lunch, hot tea or soup depending on the time of year, and drink plenty of water as it is thirsty work tending the land. Take plenty of breaks
- Try to have fun and enjoy the experience; it may be physically hard work – but you don't have to pay a monthly gym fee

Accidents do happen

- Take your time and tread carefully!

# Lost the Plot

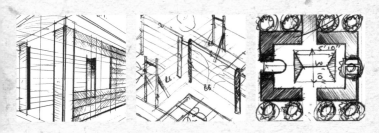

# Get creative – design your layout

**TASK ONE:** Being a successful fruit and veg grower takes a considerable amount of early planning and research as well as the hard work on site. It's a long-term investment, so it's worth the effort. Hopefully you'll have some idea of the crops you want to grow and the fruit trees and bushes to plant. This will aid you when designing the layout of your plot in how it's going to take shape: paths, shed, polytunnel, chicken coop, compost bins – possibly raised beds or straight rows, plus that fruit orchard. Get creative and sketch out your ideas – you could even win the Best Plot accolade. It is with this plan you can set out some achievable goals over the next few seasons. They are targets to achieve – your allotment resolutions. Even if you intend to sow and grow directly into the freshly cleared ground that day, you will still need to record and plan ahead – dividing your plot for the purpose of rotating your crops on a yearly cycle.

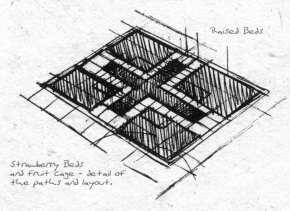

Strawberry Beds and Fruit Cage - detail of the paths and layout.

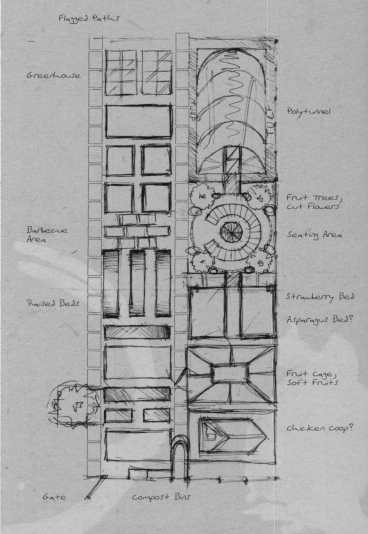

Flagged Paths

Greenhouse

Polytunnel

Fruit Trees, Cut Flowers

Barbecue Area

Seating Area

Raised Beds

Strawberry Bed

Asparagus Bed?

Fruit Cage, Soft Fruits

Chicken coop?

Gate          Compost Bins

**TASK TWO:** With an overgrown plot such as this, you need to clear the vegetation first. This is done front to back down to ground level. It will give you the blank canvas for your design. It also reveals how the last tenant worked the land and may give an indication of what veggies they may have grown. If it reveals a bed of potatoes here with a structure of canes there, take a note because you don't want to be planting the same crop in that place again for a few seasons to come. This is called crop rotation and is important in order to stop disease building up in the soil (see page 156).

# We found the
# usual suspects...

...a bath tub, greenhouse frames with carpets to match, not to forget the exercise bike!

## TASK THREE:

# COVER

Use whatever is available in order to stop the germination of seeds and the regrowth of vegetation. Black plastic is ideal for this as it excludes all light. Make sure you anchor it down with bricks to keep it from blowing away, as most allotment sites are in open, exposed areas.

If you don't have an incinerator, set aside an area for a fire pit to burn the rubbish as you clear the plot. A fire will destroy all the subsoil culture required for healthy crops, so keep this in mind. For those not so confident starting a fire, paraffin from a local petrol station or DIY store will make light work of this. Remember, paraffin is an oil substance, so if you use a fire pit, make sure to bag up and skip the waste – don't think this waste ash is useful potash. DO NOT use this ash as a soil improver, as it will contain all manner of nasty ingredients and rule out any chance of growing your veggies using organic principles.

**A point worth noting.** If you are thinking of growing your veg with organic principles in mind, think twice about using old carpets to cover cleared ground. Many people do, but it is a synthetic material that will leach chemicals into the soil over time.

## Clearing your plot

**TASK FOUR:** On our site, we have a skip and a communal composting area for weeds. Burn whatever you can, but pay attention to what the site rule book (which you should have been given when taking on the tenancy) says about this, as some allotment sites only allow fires on Sundays. Compost and skip the rest. Recycle metals and dispose of any chemicals in the correct manner. You may be fortunate to unearth and reuse stuff from the previous tenant: flag stones, bricks, timber and black plastic – even a bath tub can make a nice planter for the rhubarb. Keep and put to one side – they may come in useful at a later stage as you become more socially aware of what allotmenteering is all about.

**Reuse and recycle!**

## A blank canvas

**TASK FIVE**: After a few weekends of hard labour or paid hired help, the top growth should be cut back and disposed of with areas of the plot now under cover. Run a guideline to the boundary of your plot. If the boundary is unclear, get the committee to approve where you have set the guide – this will stop any disputes later. Edge with a spade to one spit (the depth equal to the spade length of the blade). It gives a neat edge to your plot but more importantly gives you an indication of what lies beneath – how entrenched the root systems are from the possible years of neglect. It will also give an insight into the spadework to follow and an indication whether you have inherited what was the community dumping ground at some point in its history. If you start unearthing all kinds of ironmongery, rubble, tin cans and any other rubbish you don't want to grow your fruit and veg in, it all has to come out and off the plot!

The condition of the soil front to back on your plot may also change. You could find it's sandy soil at one end and heavy clay at the other. Again, make notes and highlight these areas on your site plan. Later you can come back to these notes, test the soil and see how it needs improving.

**From now on, it's about the condition of the soil you have on your plot, how to improve it and how to keep it in good health.**

**After all, the soil is the key feature for growing fruit and veg and, as they say, you are what you eat!**

# Lost the Plot

## YEAR 1

### February

**Dirty Hands**

# Ask for HELP

Your friends, family, colleagues, neighbours.
Just don't expect the wife to dig the lot!

# Dirty Hands

## Cultivating the land once the plot has been cleared of the top vegetation is the next step. You could choose to excavate, rotavate or just dig the soil with a spade.

**Digging with a spade: sounds easy...** But, do you go for a no-dig method of growing your fruit and veg, or dig/double-dig, even trench-dig approach? Whole chapters could be dedicated to each of these subjects. New research now shows that a no-dig method creates less harm to the subsoil culture and structure, as well as to the insects and bacteria needed for healthy soil. However, don't take this as an excuse not to put spadework effort in now! This only applies to cultivated arable land, so this approach is for future growing seasons once you're established.

If, like us, you've climbed all over the entire site in order to clear it in the first place, adding to the compaction of the soil, along with the fact that you might have to cut down some triffid-sized bramble bushes, then this indicates your soil has not been worked for some time. In our case, we needed to double-dig the plot to clear the root systems and aerate the soil. This aids the structure, exposes any pests to the helpful wildlife around your plot, and brings to the surface any soil-borne disease to the harsh autumn or winter weather. This whole process of digging and weeding is a side effect you'll have to learn to love when growing your own veggies.

Lost the Plot

# 70x15ft

## That's over 1000sq ft of growing space and this is only a half plot!

Dig, Weed, Dig, Weed, Dig, Weed, Dig, Weed, Dig, Weed, Dig, Weed, Dig, Weed, Dig, Weed, Dig, Weed, Dig, Weed –
Tea break anyone?

## Dig, Weed, Dig, Weed

When we took on our allotment, we had no idea what we would be involved in, so we had no real plan as to what was required for its maintenance and upkeep. We cleared the site of rubbish with the help of a few huge bonfires, marked out the boundary and started to dig, dig, dig – front to back.

I read many wonderful books about when to sow the seeds and expect to harvest the delicious-looking fruit and vegetables. However, none illustrated the sheer hard work involved or the amount of hours you need to commit, or indicated how long it would take to achieve a fully cleared, dug and weeded plot. They illustrated the romance of growing your own, an illusion of how easy it is, which we felt under pressure to achieve.

Please don't confuse gardening at home with growing your own on an allotment site. It's a far cry from your perfect manicured back garden, which is an extension of your living space. If you have only ever grown fruit and veg in pots, be under no illusion. Taking on a plot can come as a shock, especially if you're thrown in at the deep end like we were. An allotment is, for all intents and purposes, a working site – with emphasis on the working part. Don't be put off by my straightforward blunt approach here. It's wonderfull growing your own fruit and veg but it can be a real slog in the early months so keep motivated.

Some weeds have roots that can grow over 2ft in length

## 2ft

Make sure that you remove the entire root down to the very tip; otherwise you'll be digging out the same weed in a few months' time.

Tea break anyone?

## Overload

**Do not overload yourself with the idea of digging your entire plot within a few weeks!**

It will take many, many months and the passing of seasons, even years, to cultivate single-handed. Lure friends and family with the promise of fresh goodies come harvest time  or put on an allotment barbecue party as a reward for a few hours' work or a weekend of labour.

If you have planned the layout for your allotment as suggested, and given some thought to the method of growing and to your choice of fruit and veg, you can set goals and achievable projects. For example, building strawberry beds, putting up a polytunnel or constructing a fruit cage, laying the paths or planting fruit trees.

**The allotment calendar is a 12-month cycle.** Depending on the time of year when you have taken on your plot, tasks are always at hand, weather permitting. Typically, the spring and summer months are frenetic with the preparation for sowing and planting. Don't miss out! Thoroughly clear and cultivate small designated areas and construct raised beds if desired. Weather permitting, sow your seeds to achieve a crop in your first growing season. As the summer harvest comes to an end, autumn is the time of year to plant fruit trees and fruit bushes. It is also the ideal season for more general-purpose jobs and DIY tasks, such as putting up that shed, building more raised beds and the compost bin. Continue to dig and weed into the winter months as the weather allows, slowly reclaiming the land back into good order.

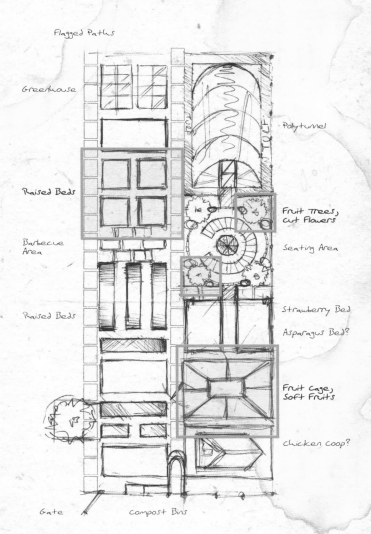

Flagged Paths

Greenhouse

Polytunnel

Raised Beds

Fruit Trees, Cut Flowers

Barbecue Area

Seating Area

Raised Beds

Strawberry Bed

Asparagus Bed?

Fruit Cage, Soft Fruits

Chicken Coop?

Gate

Compost Bins

**Decide which areas on your plan are to be cultivated first.**

The design and layout of our allotment has a very ordered and controlled fashion because of the raised bed system we have adopted. This may not be to everyone's taste and you may question this approach as too uniformed for an informal working space. However, for a busy family, everything is about time or task management. This includes self-sufficiency. Look at how to manage the whole exercise of plot cultivation into small achievable goals that will give results and keep you interested. Your design may be vastly different from ours. **Take time to look around at your neighbouring plots for good (and bad) examples and talk to your fellow plotholders for advice and tips on what works and any pitfalls to avoid.**

# Think twice!

It could be that you have taken on a plot with mature trees, perennials and shrub gardens established by the previous owner. In the winter months, you could mistake these trees for non-fruiting varieties, so think twice about removing them – come the summer you could have an abundance of fruit for very little effort.
I only mention this having seen a fellow plot neighbour remove a whole bed of asparagus, be it all too late – which would have taken many, many years to establish, only for them to be so disappointed come the spring, when a few remaining crowns pushed up their cherished shoots.

Shrubs and flowers will attract the helpful wildlife to the plot. Ladybirds love aphids and robins eat anything grubbish. You may even get a hedgehog, the organic remover of slugs and snails. Bees will pollinate your fruit and vegetables ensuring a good yield to follow.

If you are not sure about any of the plants or trees on your plot, ask the wise on the site for advice. You'll get an education from their lifetime of experience, which you'll not find in any book.

# Bring on the summer!

# Lost the Plot

### Year 1

## May

## Trial and Error

# Trial and Error

**At last, the fun can start! The warmer days mean seeds can be sown and the nurturing of your young veggies makes the hard work of the past few months a distant memory.**

Most seed packets have a description about the particular vegetable and when to sow – either undercover or directly into the ground. Some packets will give instructions about the type of compost to use to get them off to a good start, how to look after them, when to plant and, more importantly, when to harvest. If you have followed the tasks in the previous chapters, you should by now have areas of your plot cleared and cultivated ready in anticipation.

Each seed packet will give a use-by date and the number of seeds within. This date is important, so keep an eye on it. Don't use older seeds as you'll get poor results.

**Most seeds are supplied as:**
F1/F2 Hybrid, Organic, RHS approved or awarded merit, and varieties that are resistant or tolerant to disease. It may be worthwhile choosing the resistant varieties to begin with in order to get a good first season's crop under your belt, gain experience and build from there. They will still taste out of this world compared to your supermarket-bought vegetables.

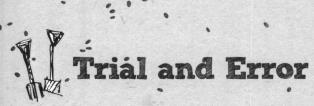

The whole ethos of 'grow your own' was new to us and it was very much a case of trial and error. Many illustrate how easy it is to grow your own – but don't expect to have green thumbs until you're no longer green behind the ears!

## Season One

In your first growing season, don't let your excitement and enthusiasm run away with you – it may lead you to grow veg without any real common sense and this will become all too evident in a few months' time. For instance, having studied the packets, we sowed all the seeds into neat straight lines several rows deep! All 800 lettuce seeds in the packet in our case. Or, after building an amazing cane structure to support the runner beans, we even planted both packets with 20 beans in each. We later learnt that each plant produces around fifty pounds in weight – that's 2000lbs of beans. Nothing short of a commercial scale!

Growing fruit and veg is relatively easy and straightforward in parts, but it's a real education when it comes to providing fresh produce to feed your family. With no one to teach or guide us, we had no real concept of what that actually takes to achieve.

For example, when you go to the supermarket, you don't buy a dozen cabbages and a 55lb bag of spuds in any weekly shop. So how do you relate the weekly shop to the amount of seeds in each packet or to how many runner bean seeds you need to sow in order to bring a constant supply of tasty fresh vegetables to the table every week, all year long?

Just how much lettuce can one family eat?

# Lost the Plot

## From plot to plate

The skill you are learning on the allotment is called crop husbandry; it is the management and cultivation of crops and animals for that matter. It's farm management but on a micro scale.

The more time-served you become, the more trials you'll face and the more success you'll achieve – it's with this time-served knowledge and some hard graft that you will ensure a constant supply of fresh veggies from plot to plate.

# Successional sowing

One of the key ingredients to self-sufficiency for the family table is successional sowing. Each seed packet gives an indication of when to sow and over what period of time – usually over a few months (see figure 1). However, if you have access to a greenhouse or a sunny window ledge, you can extend this by a few weeks at the beginning of the season. With a polytunnel you could even extend the British growing season by up to a few months – which means more veg to harvest! To put it in context with the weekly shop, sow a few seeds each week or every other week. It's the process of sowing few and often over the sowing period that is the key here. **Do not sow all the seeds at once.**

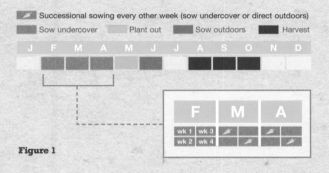

| | | | | | | | | | | | |
|---|---|---|---|---|---|---|---|---|---|---|---|
| ![] Successional sowing every other week (sow undercover or direct outdoors) | | | | | | | | | | | |
| ![] Sow undercover | | Plant out | | Sow outdoors | | | | Harvest | | | |

| J | F | M | A | M | J | J | A | S | O | N | D |
|---|---|---|---|---|---|---|---|---|---|---|---|

| F | M | A |
|---|---|---|
| wk 1 | wk 3 | |
| wk 2 | wk 4 | |

**Figure 1**

For example, the potato. You don't buy a year's supply in one go. Neither do you sow a year's supply or harvest it in one go. By design, nature has engineered this crop so different varieties can be sown successively in order to keep you in a good crop over the duration of the growing season. The potato family is divided into earlies, seconds and lates. Earlies are started off at the beginning of the season and lates mature towards the end; it's simple really.

Keep in mind that some vegetable seeds take longer to germinate than others and not all veg are suited to this method. So read the packets and do some research into the crops you sow.

It's also worth keeping in mind the quantity each veg will produce and the amount of space available on your plot in which to grow them. The 40 runner beans that we sowed didn't take up a great deal of space – because they grow upwards, but we would never have guessed they would produce such a vast quantity.

As with potatoes, each seed – depending on the fertility of your soil – will produce about a 5lb bag that you would buy with the weekly shop. So, with a little thought beforehand, you could guesstimate how many seeds you need to sow in order to keep the family in a supply of fresh spuds over the year.

Of course, this is not an exact science. Good and bad weather, soil conditions and pests all play their part in the quality of your produce, so sow a few extra – one for the family and one for nature. With the law of averages, you should break even. If you do have an abundance, the chances are your friends and family will appreciate any goodies and you will receive plenty of praise in return.

## Defend your veg!

Don't let all your hard work get eaten by slugs or pigeons. They see your plot as the best table in the house – Michelin star fine-dining. They just need a glass of indigestion salts to help aid their upset stomachs after the over-indulgence on all of your wonderful greens. They may even ask for room service if you are happy to oblige!

## Name that tune

Some gardeners see CDs as an inexpensive way to deter the pigeons. But pigeons soon learn to check their reflections in these shiny mirrors – just to make sure they haven't spilt anything while dining out at your expense! Don't rely on CDs as your only line of defence as we did.

It's a costly exercise.

We touched on vandalism earlier, but pigeons are the real heartbreakers here. They have no respect and will happily and indiscriminately destroy a whole crop of young seedlings when your back is turned. **Vandals!**

SUNFLOWER 'RUSSIAN GIANT'

## Spacing

Some veg grow very tall and need supporting, while others grow downwards into the soil. Then there are the crops growing above the surface, which have a huge display of foliage. Pay attention to the spacing requirement for each vegetable on the seed packet when sowing or planting. Correct spacing aids a healthy plant and can stop disease and pests from spreading.

We planted all the courgette plants that germinated. We were buying them every week in the supermarket, as we have done for years, but had no idea how prolific a single plant could be.

# Undercover

Our first big investments on the plot were these two 6ft x 8ft polycarbonate greenhouses. I say big investment – we actually dropped lucky at a large DIY store when they were priced up at £50 each. At that price we got two, but had to stand our ground at the checkout and endure the embarrassment of the rather large queue that formed when the polite girl informed me they did not sell greenhouses for £50.

The manager got involved, head office got involved over the phone, the warehouse manager responsible for stock control got involved and the queue got even bigger. But a price ticket is a price ticket and after much debate, we came away with what felt like the bargain of the century.

Once the site was cleared and raked flat the bases were levelled with bricks positioned every few feet and in each corner. The frame and panels slid together with ease and both greenhouses were completed over a long weekend.

The structures are watertight, but not perfectly sealed at the joints where the window panels meet on the aluminium frame. This is OK for our purpose, as we never intended to heat them – glass is far better suited to that. You will also need a small foot ladder or sturdy chair for this kind of job.

Sowing seeds under cover can give you those extra few weeks at the beginning of the season in order to get a head start. If you are thinking of purchasing a greenhouse, keep in mind the pros and cons of glass and polycarbonate. Do your research – my main concern was having children on the plot, and Maya did slam the door shut as soon as it was hinged. Thank goodness polycarbonate is almost unbreakable.

## Manure

It's worth giving a small mention now about soil management and conditioning; however, I will cover this in more detail later. **If you are going to get a delivery of manure to the plot, three ton is more than adequate for your first season and expect to pay about £35.**

I make this point only because I have seen first hand new plotholders order 10 tons of the stuff, ready to collapse when a 35ton lorry turns up with the delivery!

Remember, weeds don't need any nurturing or feeding to aid their development. In the picture above, this path was dug and weeded – but not covered. Within a few weeks in the summer, the weed had returned.

## DIY skills

Part of the fun of having an allotment is the very fact you can build stuff from scratch once you have collected all the raw materials needed.

In the next chapter, I take allotment DIY to the next level as I begin to learn more about how dedicated you have to become when growing your own veg and I see raised beds and their orderly fashion as an aid to our success.

# Lost the Plot

## YEAR 1

### November

Raising the Bed

A bed waiting to be filled that's gonna take a lot of dirt!

# Raising the Bed

With a little trial and error and a season under our belts, the excitement of what we can potentially achieve from the oncoming seasons keeps me busy over the winter months – a time when most have put their plots to bed.

**Autumn is finally here; the weather turns, the days are short, and for most the allotment is an uninspiring place at this time of year – especially if you are new to it all.** As the growing season comes to a close, the door of opportunity opens with DIY tasks to complete. Reviewing your plot plan made earlier, now is the time to build those raised beds and the compost bins, or to put up the shed. These easy-to-achieve tasks will keep you motivated over the autumn, winter months and into the spring.

Sourcing materials for the kitchen garden is a very conscious undertaking, especially if you are growing organically. Again, it's about recycling and reducing the impact on the environment around you – your personal carbon footprint. Depending on how your garden grows, most materials can be obtained free, but for the self-sufficient veg grower, some investment, one way or the other will have to be made. I have found the internet is a great place to search for all things recycled. With websites like **freecycle** and **ebay** you can find almost anything you require locally and have it delivered directly to your plot.

## Lost the Plot

With this in mind we needed a manageable solution with regards to the size of the plot and the actual amount of time we could, as a family, spare on a daily or weekly basis.

After the season of 'trial and error', we are now beginning to understand what we have taken on and the process involved in providing veggies from plot to plate. Commitment is required in order to raise vegetables from seed and to keep to the schedule of watering and sowing, which you have to incorporate into your daily routine in the summer months.

The one thing really evident in the summer months was how quickly the weeds can reclaim areas of worked land in only a matter of weeks. With the scale of the plot and only hand tools to work with, miss a week or two of hoeing on the plot and you're in big trouble.

This illustrates my point about planning and designing your plot layout before sowing and planting.

FILL LEVEL

3ft

10"

2ft

The beds have been constructed then positioned around the plot over the top of the over-wintering leeks and are dividing crop beds from the season of 'trial and error'. I now have veg growing where the paths are to be. Note how the beds have not been filled yet and this will have to wait until these crops have been harvested.

If you're working on the plot over the
winter months, take a flask – plenty of hot
drinks or soup – and wrap up warm. It can get
bitter cold, and, as a lot of sites are in open areas,
the wind chill factor can make it feel arctic.

## Get it nailed!

Trying to grow your own veg all year round is a full-time job by its very nature – so dividing the plot up into small manageable areas or raised beds is the key here to success, plus a visual aid for crop rotation. Don't be afraid to lose ground on your plot to a good network of wide paths suitable to run a wheelbarrow.

It may seem like a false economy at first (after all, you could grow veg there), but well-constructed paths will reduce your workload in the long term even though it is a lot of effort initially to lay them.

If you do decide to go down this path, it is a good idea to have your plot plan on hand to indicate where the beds are to be situated. It should also give a good indication of the individual bed sizes. Constructing the beds is the easy part here.

In our case, cutting lengths to 3ft boards for each of the ends, a couple of 3" nails hammered into each corner to join up the 13ft boards – the beds are completed. Simple! Placed equal distance apart (leaving about 2ft between for the paths). Very neat. It was at this point we realised they did not sit level and stood about 10" above the ground – **empty.**

The trouble with having a raised bed system is the simple fact you have to fill them with soil

## Advantages

The very concept of a raised bed is by its nature to raise the 'ground level' with material of your choice. This works especially well if you are unlucky enough to have poor soil on your plot.

**The advantages of the raised bed:**

- easy management of its contents
- it aids drainage, depending on how high you construct them
- in early spring they can warm up quicker than the natural ground level
- thus earlier sowing of seeds and plants
- they look neat and tidy
- if you have planned a layout with paths wide enough, you can reach the middle of the bed
- avoiding soil compaction as you don't have to stand on the soil within the bed itself.

They are also ultra-easy to maintain once constructed and filled. If you build a few larger beds, keep a length of board to one side to stand on when weeding or sowing, as this will spread your weight avoiding soil compaction.

The earlier tenants on our plot had created natural raised beds. This is the same principle we want to employ – except we are just framing ours with timber boards.

The natural raised bed consists of creating a ditch around the growing plot and heaping the soil from these ditches onto the bed – thus raising its height. Each year compost and manure is piled on top of the growing area and the ditches become the paths surrounding them. This meant our plot was very uneven and our raised beds were up to half a foot off the ground in places – so we needed to level the ground in order for them to sit squarely and flat.

## Disadvantage

The big disadvantage of a raised bed system, after the initial cost and energy required to construct, is filling them. You can purchase topsoil or compost by the ton and again the internet is a good place to start searching for a local supplier. If, like us, you need to keep an eye on the monthly budget, this is a lavish expense.

## Fill 'em

With a dozen beds constructed and needing to be filled, but not having the cash to spend on a couple of tons of soil or compost, you could think it was a pointless exercise to build a raised bed system in the first place. However, the unforeseen part of this whole exercise came in the extra workload of levelling the raised beds and the surrounding network of undulating paths. The topsoil excavated was put to good use and thankfully solved the problem of filling the empty beds at no extra monetary cost. With the warm weather on its way, it only takes a few weeks for the weeds to undo a lot of the hard work. Lessons learnt from the previous season of 'trial and error' tell me the next task is to cover and pin the paths with the breathable weed-suppressing fabric – again sourced from the internet. One hundred meters costs about £40.

Variations in the shapes and sizes of your raised beds will give you greater scope when it comes to choosing which fruit and veg to grow. For instance, sweetcorn is planted in blocks, as opposed to rows, and squashes will enjoy the extra space provided by the larger beds.

The whole process illustrated in this chapter of constructing beds, filling with soil and levelling the paths took around four months, from the beginning of autumn until the end of winter. Luckily, I was very motivated by the success and reward from the previous season, which encouraged me to commit the time, effort and energy.

**I'm not endorsing this level of commitment, afterall, I am a self-confessed allotment junkie!**

## Coldframe

Most allotment sites have a never-ending supply of glass and our plot was no exception. Raised beds can easily double up as a coldframe for no extra effort just by placing glass panes on top of them. This is ideal for hardening-off young plants or for growing more exotic fruits or veg by offering the extra warmth. If you have children on the plot, be careful when using glass for any purpose – in fact I would discourage the use of it altogether as the risk of a breakage is too great. There are some really good plastic alternatives available on the market – just look at our greenhouses for instance.

**Having come so far in the last 12 months, we are looking forward to bumper crops in season two!**

# Lost the Plot

the

# YEAR 2

## March

Summer of Love

The path to **SUCCESS** and not a weed to be seen

# Summer of Love

Season two is almost upon us and the allotment is coming back to life. It's good to meet up again with friends made the year before. Ahead is our first full growing season and, like everyone else, we are keen to start off on a good footing.

**Spring on the allotment is possibly the busiest time of all – renewed energy and resolutions after the winter hibernation.** Preparation, preparation, preparation is the key. We plan what to grow and where to sow. Seeds and plants ordered via the internet arrive in the post and we take frequent visits to the garden centre to top up supplies. It all adds to the excitement!

Hopefully, you turned the soil in the autumn before putting the plot to bed. If not, you will probably have some spadework to do now in order to get the plot shipshape over the next few weeks. Because I was on the plot over the winter months, we were well ahead of the game at this point and felt like seasoned pros – especially since our neighbours noticed all the effort put in over the past few months and heaped praise upon us! However, as I have learnt and continue to learn, hard landscaping is the easy part when it comes to growing your own!

Grow bags purchased ready to fill the greenhouse boarders are the ideal medium, or just plant directly into the bag itself.

With the boarders now full and ready for plants, sink pots or empty plastic bottles with the base cut off dotted around the bed. This will aid when watering during the hot summer months, water directly into these and the water will sink in at the root level when the top soil can bake into a dry impervious crust in the heat.

## Season Two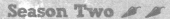

With the spring season now in full flight, the greenhouses are washed and thoroughly cleaned and structures of wigwam canes built for the oncoming flood of beans. This season we have opted for a wigwam structure after last season's lesson, and plant only half a dozen runner bean plants this time around. However, having never grown tomatoes in a greenhouse before, and having read the instructions and researched 'ring culture' – **I find I am still making the classic mistakes of quantity over quality.**

A greenhouse or polytunnel is the perfect environment for raising plants from seed. After the slugs got so many of our young veggies sown directly into the soil last season, this is the method for us!

## Test the soil pH

Spring is the ideal time to test your soil for its pH reading before sowing or planting out your crop. Several kits are available, some more scientific and accurate than others. Ours is a probe that is directed to root depth and removes any fear of the chemistry set. Below is a list of the most common grown fruit and vegetables with an indication of their soil pH requirements, with most valued between 5.5 and 7.5.

| | |
|---|---|
| Ultra acidic | <3.5 |
| Extreme acidity | 3.5 – 4.4 |
| Very strong acidity | 4.5 – 5.0 |
| Strong acidity | 5.1 – 5.5 |
| Moderate acidity | 5.6 – 6.0 |
| Slight acidity | 6.1 – 6.5 |
| **Neutral** | **6.6 – 7.3** |
| Slightly alkaline | 7.4 – 7.8 |
| Moderately alkaline | 7.9 – 8.4 |
| Strongly alkaline | 8.5 – 9.0 |
| Very strong alkalinity | >9.0 |

### Key

pH (Potential of Hydrogen) scale is the measurement of the level of acidity or alkalinity in the soil water in which 7.0 is neutral.

**Vegetables**

| | |
|---|---|
| Artichokes | 6.5 – 7.5 |
| **Asparagus** | **6.0 – 6.8** |
| Aubergines | 6.0 – 6.5 |
| **Basil** | **5.5 – 6.5** |
| Bay | 4.5 – 8.3 |
| **Beetroot** | **6.5 – 7.0** |
| Broad Bean | 6.0 – 7.5 |
| **Broccoli** | **6.0 – 6.8** |
| Brussels sprouts | 6.0 – 7.5 |
| **Cabbage** | **6.0 – 6.8** |
| Carrot | 5.5 – 7.0 |
| **Cauliflower** | **5.5 – 7.5** |
| Celery | 6.0 – 7.0 |
| **Chilli** | **5.0 – 6.0** |
| Chives | 6.0 – 7.5 |
| **Courgette** | **6.0 – 7.5** |
| Cucumber | 5.5 – 6.8 |
| **French Bean** | **6.0 – 6.5** |
| Garlic | 6.0 – 7.0 |
| **Kale** | **6.0 – 7.5** |
| Kohl Rabi | 5.5 – 6.0 |
| **Leek** | **6.0 – 8.0** |
| Lettuce | 6.0 – 7.0 |
| **Mint** | **6.0 – 7.5** |
| Onion | 6.0 – 7.0 |
| **Parsley** | **5.0 – 5.5** |
| Pea | 5.5 – 6.8 |

| | |
|---|---|
| **Potato** | **5.0 – 6.8** |
| Pepper | 6.0 – 6.5 |
| **Pumpkin** | **6.0 – 6.5** |
| Parsnip | 6.5 – 7.0 |
| **Radish** | **6.0 – 7.0** |
| Rosemary | 6.0 – 7.5 |
| **Runner Bean** | **5.5 – 7.0** |
| Rhubarb | 5.0 – 6.8 |
| **Sage** | **5.5 – 6.5** |
| Squash | 6.0 – 6.5 |
| **Spinach** | **6.0 – 7.5** |
| Shallots | 6.2 – 6.8 |
| **Sweetcorn** | **6.0 – 6.5** |
| Swede | 5.5 – 7.0 |
| **Tomato** | **5.5 – 6.8** |
| Thyme | 6.0 – 6.7 |
| **Turnip** | **6.0 – 6.5** |

**Fruit**

| | |
|---|---|
| Blackberry | 5.0 – 6.0 |
| **Blackcurrant** | **6.0 – 8.0** |
| Blueberry | 4.5 – 5.5 |
| **Cranberry** | **4.5 – 5.0** |
| Gooseberry | 5.0 – 6.5 |
| **Melon** | **6.5 – 7.0** |
| Raspberry | 5.0 – 6.8 |
| **Redcurrant** | **5.5 – 7.0** |
| Strawberry | 5.0 – 7.5 |

Knowing the pH value of your soil helps to give you an indication of its health and whether remedy ingredients are required to balance its values, bringing it back into the neutral zone required by most vegetables.

Poor results from soil testing (at either end of the scale) may indicate soil that is prone to incubate pests and disease as the health of the soil is in question, possibly due to the lack of nutrients and oxygen required for the subsoil life cycle to thrive.

The application of manure or a dusting with lime is usually sufficient to achieve harmony and soil fertility. Note that some fruit bushes – blueberries for example – require the soil to be high in acidic content and indeed compost can be purchased formulated to this specification. Spring is the ideal time to spread well-rotted manure (stored from the season before) as the beds are empty. If applied in the autumn, the nutrients will wash away over the winter months. Manure is the perfect improver to be added to the soil before a bed of potatoes is planted. A little planning in your early months can give back big rewards later. In the meantime, a scattering of organic dried chicken pellets will add slow-releasing nutrients into the soil over the growing season.

**Remember** – a lot of vegetables don't like freshly manured ground, especially root veg, so keep this in mind (see page 156). I often see many virgin plotholders adding fresh manure at this time of year, when the seasoned plotholders are taking deliveries to store away to rot down for the following season. **Note:** fresh horse manure is high in acidity, so can burn or scorch young tender shoots if applied directly.

At this point, no manure or compost had been added to our plot – mainly because we had not planned ahead. We never thought we would progress so quickly when we took on our overgrown patch! We also had no compost bins in place – it's a must-do task for this season. Plan to get yours built as soon as you possibly can, as home or plot-cultivated compost is possibly the best ingredient you can add to your soil to keep it healthy.

**Sow-water-plant, replaces dig-weed-dig.**
At this time of year nearly every weekend is spent on the allotment – sowing seed and nurturing young plants. As the summer gets warmer, the routine of watering almost becomes a daily cycle you have to commit to.

Organic dried chicken pellet release nutrients into the soil slowly over a long period of time.

## Season Two: Lessons learned

Not to be mugged this season by the pigeons, defences are built and tender veggies covered with netting placed over half-inch rigid flex, sunk into holes drilled into the frame of the raised beds then secured by screw hooks.

At this stage, I'm covering anything that looks edible: the sweetcorn, the nursery bed and even the leeks! Be aware: it's not just the pigeons you are protecting the veg from here – cabbage white butterfly can do equal damage if only over a longer period of time.

**Remember – these little fellows are on the prowl!**
Beer traps, slug pellets, nematodes – arm yourselves with whatever weapons you see fit, the choice is yours! Remember, you have to live with your actions afterwards and not all methods of control are good for the garden.

Onion sets planted in perfect straight lines. You don't need to protect these from the pigeons but keep an eye out for any they have pulled up and push them back in. Lesson learned: they don't like strong taste or smell, so this also applies to garlic.

Within a very short period, the onion sets have grown a height and the bulbs are now beginning to swell. Make sure you are watering every day. A liquid feed will help them put on more weight.

This one bed contains about a year's supply of onions for a small-sized family. However, onion sets can be planted in the autumn and the spring, so you can always have a constant fresh supply.

One of the lessons I'm still learning in Season Two is spacing. Even having read the packet and after raising these young plants from seed, I'm still thinking of quantity not quality. This picture painfully illustrates my over enthusiasm with these cabbages.

And to think that I actually made that measuring stick!

A few weeks on and the young greenhouse veg raised from seed are ready for hardening-off. This is a process of moving them outdoors during the day and bringing them back in at night to acclimatise for about a week or so.

The potatoes are now pushing up and need earthing up to ensure none of them turn green from the sun. Green potatoes are poisonous, so bin them if you have any when it's time to harvest. When planting your seed potatoes, leave a few weeks between planting the earlies, seconds and lates, otherwise – like me – all your spuds are going to come up at the same time. See pages 156/160 for more info on planting and harvesting potatoes and manure rotation.

So far the netting is proving a success and the nursery bed is looking healthy with plants now ready to be planted into their final places.

My potatoes sown back in February in these large pots - in the greenhouse - have proven a success with a harvest of earlies weeks before any of the outdoor crop is ready for the dinner table.

## Lessons still being learned!

I have learnt a great deal in my first season of 'trial and error', and 15 months on I am by no means a skilled grower of vegetables! Here I clearly illustrate my over enthusiasm in the greenhouse and my lack of time-served knowledge.

The wheelbarrow barbecue: an allotment ritual. It gives a whole new meaning to meals on wheels!

I'm not trying to illuminate my faults for not being classically trained here - just the fact that as a novice you can expect these things to happen in the early years. Don't be put off if you get a few things wrong to start with, it's all part of the fun, however frustrating it can be at times. Whenever possible ask the wise on your allotment for help and advice – they are time-served green-fingered specialists!

what was I thinking? Thirty plants in one greenhouse. I've still a lot to learn!

This is the first time we have grown peas. I'm constructing defences against the pigeons as the earlier direct sowing had their tender growing tips pecked off by the little tinkers.

## Crop rotation

Having now grown lots of different vegetables with varying degrees of success, one key element of the crop-growing year now comes into play – and one that is important because of its cycle within the kitchen garden. The basic principle of crop rotation (see page 156) is to move around the plot groups or families of vegetables – NOT planting or sowing them in the same place over a three, four or even a five-year period. It all depends on the amount of space you have to play with. Understanding the different families the veg you grow belong to will help you when planning this important practice on the allotment.

### The different vegetable families:

| | |
|---|---|
| **Roots:** | **Carrots, Parsnips, Beetroot, Swedes, Turnips, Potatoes** |
| **Brassicas:** | **Cabbages, Cauliflowers, Broccoli, Brussels Sprouts, Kale, Spinach** |
| **Alliums:** | **Onions, Shallots, Leeks, Garlic** |
| **Legumes:** | **Peas, French Beans, Runner Beans, Broad Beans** |
| **Salads:** | **Lettuce etc** |
| **Fruiting:** | **Tomatoes, Peppers, Chillies, Aubergines** |
| **Squashes:** | **Cucumbers, Pumpkins, Courgettes, Squashes** |
| **Perennials:** | **Asparagus, Artichokes, Rhubarb** |
| **Herbs:** | **Basil, Chives, Thyme, Mint, Bay, Rosemary, Sage, Parsley etc** |

**Start taking notes of what you have sown and grown on your plot so that you can begin to plan out your rotation for the next season.**

As a rule of thumb, the vegetable cycle follows this yearly order:

**Add:  Manure (if required)**

Year 1    Potatoes and Tomatoes

Year 2    Peas, Beans and Roots:
          (Parsnips, Carrots etc, sow in Yr. 5
          OR purpose beds if space allows)

**Add:  Lime (if required)**

Year 3    Cabbage, Sprouts, Broccoli etc

Year 4    Onions, Leeks, Garlic, Lettuce,
          Sweetcorn etc (Group with Yr. 2
          if it's a three year crop rotation).

The reason for ordering the way the vegetables are planted in a prescribed sequence is two-fold:

- By rotating the crops in this way you have less chance of a build-up in soil-borne pests and diseases, thus making for healthy crops
- By the nature of the crop itself, they have different requirements and demands from the soil.

**For example:** Potatoes love manure and will grow away happily and produce a bumper harvest. Root veg, however, will find this too rich in nutrients and not taper downwards, becoming twisted and forked. The cabbage family require a much less acidic soil created by the manure and may require a dusting of lime to balance the pH of the soil before planting.

**For more information on crop and manure rotation see pages 156 and 157.**

The greenhouse is proving its worth with a bumper crop of tomatoes, aubergine and basil. Even the pot-grown hot chillies, sweet peppers, cucumbers and gherkins are enjoying the warm conditions.

French Beans

Runner Beans

Butternut

Swede

Sweetcorn

Parsnip

Cauliflower

Leeks

Broccoli

Peas

Brussels Sprout

Onions

Broad Beans

Kale

Garlic

Mangetout

Cabbage

Shallots

Potatoes

Mint

Courgette

Beetroot

Radish

# Bumper harvest

It's now July on the plot and the rewards are more than expected. With every inch of space and every raised bed full of crops, it's a delight.

The choice now for us is what to do with all the gluts of fresh vegetables. This is now our introduction to storing and preserving – yet another ingredient in the quest for self-sufficiency. It's not until this point that we realise just how unprepared we were, both in knowledge and hardware.

Jars, vinegars, sterilising equipment, a bigger freezer – storing and preserving, by its very nature, is a book in itself. So at this point, we are giving away any perishable veggies, learning how to string up the onions and garlic and freezing any gluts of beans after blanching.

With a cold beer in hand, there is satisfaction after those winter months and all that hard work. It's hard to believe that we have achieved this level of success in little over a year. The plot is now producing an abundance of fresh veggies faster than we can pick and eat.

## Annual show

Every year on our allotment site, we have an annual show organised by the site committee. The committee includes a chairperson, treasurer and other responsible folk who oversee all matters associated with the site and work really hard towards its upkeep.

The annual show is a bit of fun and pulls together the plotholders around a barbecue for a few beers and to show off those prized veggies. It's also a chance to meet the wise and the new and exchange tales of success and failure. Take time to have a look around other neighbours' plots for inspiration for the next growing season.

**Categories at the show include:**

- Best Newcomers' Plot
- Best Overall Plot
- Largest Runner Bean
- Heaviest Potato
- Heaviest Marrow
- Best Selection of Salad
- Best Selection of Vegetables
- Best Display of Flowers
- Best Made Jam and Wine
- The Funniest Vegetable

It is supposed to be a bit of fun; however, I did hear about one chap feeding his marrows Guinness to increase their size. Our own first prize, for the 'funniest vegetable', never went anywhere near Viagra! As well as the first prize, we won second for our selection of chillies and third prize for our selection of veg.

## "This is the new rock and roll"

CLASS 7

CLASS 7

NO 9

UTHERN ALLOTMENT SOCIET

ANNUAL SHOW 2009

FIRST PRIZE

CLASS Funniest vegetable

NAME.............................

Produced by
allotment
JUNKIE

## Winter veg

Although it's the height of summer, the kitchen gardener has to keep an eye on the months ahead to ensure a constant stream of fresh fruit and vegetables from the plot to the plate.

### Intercropping

As the name suggests, intercropping is just a way of growing vegetables that mature faster than the neighbouring row of veg. It's ideal for sowing salad leaves in-between your rows of winter veg, which have tenancy for up to nine months of the year and demand large areas of your plot.

### Catch-cropping

This method requires fast-growing veg, which can be planted into 'free' or 'empty' beds, as and when they become available, over the duration of the growing season and before your over-winter veg are planted out.

Early spring is the time to start thinking about sowing your winter veg. These are usually sown in pots or modules undercover to get them off to a good start – away from the prowling slugs and pigeons. Once strong enough, these young veg are planted out in the height of summer.

These hardy vegetables will sit on the plot for a long period of time before they are ready to harvest. Leeks, cabbage, Brussels sprouts and cauliflowers, all take up a lot of space where summer crops could be grown. One method to overcome this problem, especially if you have a smaller plot, is to intercrop or catch-crop your veggies.

## Season's end

The spring and summer of our Season Two have surpassed our expectations as a family. I'm now even more enthused and my eye keeps looking if the grass is greener on the other side of the fence – it's certainly very tall. Every inch of our plot has provided in one way or another and I am now thinking of next year's growing season, how to increase our yield and diversify our veg with fruits.

Like many who take on an allotment, the work load can seem too much at times and does not fit in with the modern day pace of living. This is partly why I have tried to illustrate just how much time and effort goes into the upkeep of a plot. In our case, this has played to our advantage and we asked for first refusal on the neighbouring plot on the other side of the fence, should it become available.

**Keep in mind my earlier comments about buying a shed. Those who find an allotment too much work after a couple of months could find it a costly purchase. Many tenants don't bother removing or selling it on once having resigned (or been evicted) from the plot. Remember, if you have bought a shed new, it could have cost you well over £100 for a basic 4 x 6ft, and upwards for the better constructed models.**

Paving flags, reclaimed house bricks, stone and gravel are the desired substrate required here and give a lifetime of service. Woodchip looks more rustic and is easier to lay, but it will only last a season or two before some kind of remedial work is required.

## Bricking it

Having planned the layout of the allotment, built the raised beds, levelled and covered over the paths to stop any weed growth, the next step is to lay a suitable material to the network of pathways – a job best done during the autumn season, weather permitting. You'll have more time for all the DIY work on the plot as the frenetic growing season comes to a close.

Hardcore, sharp sand, staggered rows, basket-weave or herringbone. The longevity of the paths you build is in their preparation and construction. But some may find this a little overboard for a working site. If your plot is traditional in its layout and function, it may be a good idea to edge the paths with timber to stop any overspill onto the growing patch. Because the allotment is a working environment – hard pathways are extremely functional as most sites are in open areas, vulnerable to the elements. Pathways get saturated and become muddy very quickly in the winter months, especially if you have a clay soil – making it impossible to drain away any excess water.

For my part, I just used what was available with no real cost involved other than time. The bricks were laid down in no particular fashion, other than they fitted together. I then covered over with a bag or two of small gravel to fill any gaps.

A brick pathway will add loads of charm to the overall look of your plot, but remember the allotment code of reuse and recycle. It was never our intention to lay a 'brick' pathway but, by way of good fortune, we unearthed barrow loads of them from the undergrowth on the new plot we had just taken on.

### Soak away

Clay patches or areas of compacted soil on any plot soon become large standing pools when the weather turns, and our plot is no exception. The very fact that the plot is slightly higher at one end and dips towards a focal point meant some remedial work was required in the way of a drainage pit.

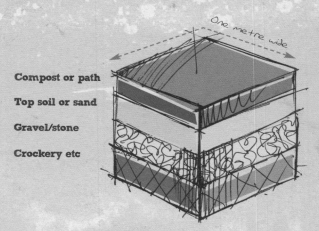

One metre wide

Compost or path

Top soil or sand

Gravel/stone

Crockery etc

A drainage pit or soakaway is simply a large hole, dug about a metre deep and as wide as you can manage. Back fill with any loose crockery, broken bricks, stones and a deep layer of gravel. A drainage hole may seem a little extreme for most people on an allotment site, especially when double-digging may relieve the problem by breaking up the surface soil. It can also be used as a system for collecting excess water into low-level storage tanks. If this appeals to you, just do a little more research into this method of water recycling.

> Whether you are a novice wanting to grow your own fruit and veg for the first time or have seasoned green fingers, whatever your ambitions are over the forthcoming growing seasons, I hope this book serves as an inspiration, but more importantly has illustrated from the word go, just what it takes to be a successful plotholder. The next few pages just go to show all the effort you put in is so rewarding and easily achievable once you get the basics right.

The self-confessed
'Allotment Junkie'

Produced by
allotment
JUNKIE

# Lost the Plot

## YEAR 2

### Grubs up!

Eat your Greens

# KALE
## DWARF GREEN CURLED

# Eat your Greens

**After all the season's hard work, it's time to enjoy the harvest from our summer of love. The abundance of our allotment-grown fruit and veg only goes to serve as an inspiration to future success.**

**For us as a family to achieve our 'summer' of self-sufficiency has taken 24 months or two growing seasons of trial and error. Over the next few pages we illustrate just a small selection of our home-grown produce.**

To make this book even more practical we've added space for your own fruit and veg planner to help you keep a record of your future success for later reference.

Note how the weather plays its role, when you added manure, tested the soil pH or suffered with potato blight. It is trial and error in the first few years as you learn. Remember that with perseverance comes the fruit of your labours.

RH
UB
AR
B

# CAULIFLOWER
## GREEN
## TREVI

# CAPSICUM
## HOT CHILLI
### AND JALAPEÑO SUMMER HEAT

NEW

EARLIES

FIRST

SECONDS

LATES

Produced by
**a**llotment
**JUNKIE**

CORN

SWEET

**SAVOY CABBAGE**

ONIONS

DWARF BEAN 'OPERA'
RUNNER BEAN 'DESIREE'
CLIMBING BEAN 'FASOLD'

# BEANS

**RUNNER : DWARF : HARICOT : CLIMBING**

CLIMBING BEAN BORLOTTO
'FIRETONGUE'

TURNIP
PURPLE TOP

# MILAN

PEAS

# MAINCROP

### MARROWFAT 'ONWARD'

SWISS CHARD

BRIGHT LIGHTS

# Notes

Keep a lookout for slugs and snails around the plot and remove by hand if growing your veggies with organic principles.

Slugs and snails are a relentless enemy of the veg grower, so try to encourage wildlife such as frogs and hedgehogs to your plot to help keep them under control

Keep a lookout for caterpillars on your brassicas. Rub them off before they mature and start to nibble. Check for the telltale signs and pick off any that have survived. Check continuously!

Produced by
a**l**lotment
JUNKIE
I grew these

FROM PLOT TO PLATE

Spring Summer Autumn Winter

**Fruit and Veg Planner**

# Useful Links

Listed below are a few helpful links to websites within the 'grow your own' community.

## Seed suppliers

www.kingsseeds.com
www.dobies.co.uk
www.allotinabox.com
www.mr-fothergills.co.uk
www.dtbrownseeds.co.uk
www.simpsonsseeds.co.uk
www.suttons.co.uk
www.thompson-morgan.com
www.marshalls-seeds.co.uk
www.unwins-seeds.co.uk
www.jungleseeds.co.uk
www.qualityseeds4less.co.uk
www.simplyseed.co.uk
www.realseeds.co.uk
www.tuckers-seeds.com

## Soil conditioners

www.mrmuck.co.uk
www.dandysgardencentre.co.uk
www.rolawn.co.uk
www.creativegardenideas.co.uk

## Pest control

www.nemasysinfo.co.uk
www.kakoi.co.uk

## Tunnels and frames

www.agriframes.co.uk
www.firsttunnels.co.uk
www.northernpolytunnels.co.uk
www.premierpolytunnels.co.uk
www.wmjames.co.uk
www.polytunnels.com
www.ferryman-polytunnels.co.uk
www.fivestarpolytunnels.co.uk

## Publications

www.growfruitandveg.co.uk
www.kitchengarden.co.uk
www.growitmag.com
www.gardenersworld.com
www.amateurgardening.com

## Organisations

www.nsalg.org.uk
www.amas.org.uk
www.nvsuk.org.uk
www.allotment.org.uk
www.sags.org.uk

## Shows and events

www.thegrowyourownshow.co.uk
www.theediblegardenshow.co.uk
www.bbcgardenersworldlive.com
www.rhs.org.uk/Shows-Events

## Education

www.my-garden-school.com
www.rhs.org.uk/Courses

## Tools

www.bulldogtools.co.uk
www.qualitygardentools.com

## Sheds

www.gardenbuildingsdirect.co.uk
www.shedstore.co.uk

## Equipment and products

www.harrodhorticultural.com
www.twowests.co.uk
www.gardening-naturally.com

## Information sites

www.rhs.org.uk
www.gardenorganic.org.uk
www.growveg.com
www.bbc.co.uk/gardening
www.gardenersheaven.co.uk
www.thehorticulturalchannel.info

## Greenhouse

www.greenhousepeople.co.uk
www.greenhousesrus.co.uk
www.isgreenhouses.co.uk

## Forums

www.chat.allotment.org.uk
www.allotments-uk.com/forum
www.growfruitandveg.co.uk/
   grapevine
www.gardenorganic.org.uk/
   members/forum

# Fruit and Veg Planner

**Variety:**

**Comments:**

**Crop Rotation - Planted in position:** A B C D : 1 2 3 4

**Notes**

**Date Sown:**         :         :

**Date Planted:**         :         :

**Rating:**   ★ ★ ★ ★ ★         /10

**Other:**

---

**Variety:**

**Comments:**

**Crop Rotation - Planted in position:** A B C D : 1 2 3 4

**Notes**

**Date Sown:**         :         :

**Date Planted:**         :         :

**Rating:**   ★ ★ ★ ★ ★         /10

**Other:**

---

**Variety:**

**Comments:**

**Crop Rotation - Planted in position:** A B C D : 1 2 3 4

**Notes**

**Date Sown:**         :         :

**Date Planted:**         :         :

**Rating:**   ★ ★ ★ ★ ★         /10

**Other:**

---

**Variety:**

**Comments:**

**Crop Rotation - Planted in position:** A B C D : 1 2 3 4

**Notes**

**Date Sown:**         :         :

**Date Planted:**         :         :

**Rating:**   ★ ★ ★ ★ ★         /10

**Other:**

# Fruit and Veg Planner

**Variety:**

**Comments:**

**Crop Rotation - Planted in position: A B C D : 1 2 3 4**     **Other:**

**Notes**

**Date Sown:**    :    :

**Date Planted:**    :    :

**Rating:** ★★★★    /10

---

**Variety:**

**Comments:**

**Crop Rotation - Planted in position: A B C D : 1 2 3 4**     **Other:**

**Notes**

**Date Sown:**    :    :

**Date Planted:**    :    :

**Rating:** ★★★★★    /10

---

**Variety:**

**Comments:**

**Crop Rotation - Planted in position: A B C D : 1 2 3 4**     **Other:**

**Notes**

**Date Sown:**    :    :

**Date Planted:**    :    :

**Rating:** ★★★★★    /10

---

**Variety:**

**Comments:**

**Crop Rotation - Planted in position: A B C D : 1 2 3 4**     **Other:**

**Notes**

**Date Sown:**    :    :

**Date Planted:**    :    :

**Rating:** ★★★★★    /10

# Fruit and Veg Planner

Variety: _____

Comments: _____

Date Sown: ___ : ___ : ___

Date Planted: ___ : ___ : ___

Rating: ★ ★ ★ ★ ★ ___/10

Crop Rotation - Planted in position:  A B C D : 1 2 3 4        Other: _____

Notes

_____

---

Variety: _____

Comments: _____

Date Sown: ___ : ___ : ___

Date Planted: ___ : ___ : ___

Rating: ★ ★ ★ ★ ★ ___/10

Crop Rotation - Planted in position:  A B C D : 1 2 3 4        Other: _____

Notes

_____

---

Variety: _____

Comments: _____

Date Sown: ___ : ___ : ___

Date Planted: ___ : ___ : ___

Rating: ★ ★ ★ ★ ★ ___/10

Crop Rotation - Planted in position:  A B C D : 1 2 3 4        Other: _____

Notes

_____

---

Variety: _____

Comments: _____

Date Sown: ___ : ___ : ___

Date Planted: ___ : ___ : ___

Rating: ★ ★ ★ ★ ★ ___/10

Crop Rotation - Planted in position:  A B C D : 1 2 3 4        Other: _____

Notes

_____

# Fruit and Veg Planner

Variety:

Comments:

Date Sown:                    :          :

Date Planted:                 :          :

Rating:    ★ ★ ★ ★          /10

Crop Rotation - Planted in position:  A B C D : 1 2 3 4        Other:

Notes

---

Variety:

Comments:

Date Sown:                    :          :

Date Planted:                 :          :

Rating:    ★ ★ ★ ★ ★          /10

Crop Rotation - Planted in position:  A B C D : 1 2 3 4        Other:

Notes

---

Variety:

Comments:

Date Sown:                    :          :

Date Planted:                 :          :

Rating:    ★ ★ ★ ★ ★          /10

Crop Rotation - Planted in position:  A B C D : 1 2 3 4        Other:

Notes

---

Variety:

Comments:

Date Sown:                    :          :

Date Planted:                 :          :

Rating:    ★ ★ ★ ★ ★          /10

Crop Rotation - Planted in position:  A B C D : 1 2 3 4        Other:

Notes

**Variety:** _____

**Comments:** _____

**Date Sown:** ___ : ___ : ___

**Date Planted:** ___ : ___ : ___

**Rating:** ★ ★ ★ ★ ★    /10

**Crop Rotation - Planted in position:** A B C D : 1 2 3 4      **Other:**

**Notes**
_____
_____

**Variety:** _____

**Comments:** _____

**Date Sown:** ___ : ___ : ___

**Date Planted:** ___ : ___ : ___

**Rating:** ★ ★ ★ ★ ★    /10

**Crop Rotation - Planted in position:** A B C D : 1 2 3 4      **Other:**

**Notes**
_____
_____

**Variety:** _____

**Comments:** _____

**Date Sown:** ___ : ___ : ___

**Date Planted:** ___ : ___ : ___

**Rating:** ★ ★ ★ ★ ★    /10

**Crop Rotation - Planted in position:** A B C D : 1 2 3 4      **Other:**

**Notes**
_____
_____

**Variety:** _____

**Comments:** _____

**Date Sown:** ___ : ___ : ___

**Date Planted:** ___ : ___ : ___

**Rating:** ★ ★ ★ ★ ★    /10

**Crop Rotation - Planted in position:** A B C D : 1 2 3 4      **Other:**

**Notes**
_____
_____

## Example

If you have taken the time to complete your veg planner (as below) and made notes, you'll have a great source of reference come next season as to what worked and what did not on your plot. Allotment plots can vary from one end of the site to the next and, indeed, from end to end on your very own plot. If you are new to growing your own veg, fully understanding your plot could take many growing seasons, so this will aid in the understanding of it – it's just good house-keeping at the end of the day.

| Variety: | LETTUCE - 'Tom Thumb' | Date Sown: | '23 : 05 : 09 |
|---|---|---|---|
| Comments: | Sown direct into the soil, in rows | Date Planted: | : : |
| 02/08/09 - Next time don't sow the whole packet in one go | | Rating: ★★★★★ | 8 /10 |
| Crop Rotation - Planted in position: A B C D : 1 2 3 4 | Other: | | Salad Bed |
| Notes | 'Great crop, crisp and nice'. Slugs luv 'em too! | | |
| | 15/07/09 - Need beer traps next season or slug pellets - maybe start off in modules. | | |

Some veg growers have had the same plot for decades; they know what grows well and grow what they like the most. Even if you don't see yourself as a long-term tenant, passing on this kind of material to the next guardian of the plot would be invaluable. So why not pass on this book (via the committee) to the next plotholder as a source for them?

**With fingers crossed, next season will be just as good, if not better, as you'll be a year wiser and fitter down on the veg plot.**

**Allotment Site Name:**

**Plot Number:**

Lost the Plot

YEAR 2

December

Extra Cold

-17°C

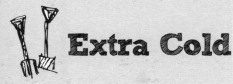

# Extra Cold

**After a very wet November, December on the plot is cold and quiet with hardly a soul to be seen – other than Jack Frost for company. It really feels like a place of exile, especially when the Siberian snow hits in January.**

Many people put their plots to bed over the winter months – now I know why. I must be insane going down the plot when it's this cold!

In 2009 we witnessed the temperature at Woodford in Manchester plummet to −17°C and in the summer months rise to record highs.

The one thing about growing your own, especially if your aim is self-sufficiency, is how big a part the weather begins to play in your daily life. As you become more aware of the changing seasons and your environment, the more you become culturally aware of climate change and its effects on even your small plot – nevermind on a global scale.

Lost the Plot

Work on the allotment comes to a standstill in conditions like this. You only need to venture on site if you have any livestock, chickens or rabbits (for which you are responsible). I do recall a couple getting metaphorically kicked off the site by the committee for not tending to their flock over this season of goodwill.

**A word of caution:** If you do decide to venture onto the allotment in weather conditions like this, be very careful! Most plots are working sites – which means they can be hazardous in winter, especially with snow on the ground. Take a mobile phone with you and don't forget to tell someone you're off down the allotment for a couple of hours. Don't be surprised if they think you have **lost the plot.**

As this is the first winter the polycarbonate greenhouses have faced, and having had 10cm of snowfall in the past 12 hours, I'm keen to brush down the deposit – not knowing if they can withstand the weight of the snow.

## Daddy's little helper

With fun to be had in the snow, Maya is extra-keen to come down to the plot and help daddy. Making snow angels and clearing the paths with a 'ho ho ho and it's off to work we go' – it makes for a wonderful afternoon. Just the two of us, having quality family-time together on the plot.

With no veggies to harvest as the ground is frozen solid, I'm not sure if even the hardiest of winter leeks could survive these Siberian conditions.

**We'll just have to wait and see...**

**Come on the spring!**

# Lost
## the
# Plot
# PART
# ONE

Sick Days

# HOSEPIPE BAN IN OPERATION

142 | Lost the Plot - Sick Days

# Sick Days

**Floods, 90mph winds, −10°C, 2ft of snow, drought, disease and destruction. I'm not writing a film script! This is the 'finger of God' kind of stuff that allotment growers all over the nation have faced in the past 12 months.**

**In contradiction to the eight-week hosepipe ban in the summer of 2010, freak stormy rains flooded many parts of the UK.**

As illustrated, the weather plays its hand when it comes to growing your own fruit and veg. Colder winters are now the norm, with very poor, wet summers and warmer, dry spring days.

As well as poor weather to contend with, you'll learn about all manner of fruit and vegetable debilitating diseases. Not to mention the good, the bad and the ugly of insects and pests on your plot. Over the next few pages, we look at just a few of the likely contenders you'll face in the first year or so on the allotment. This is not a complete A – Z of pests and diseases, merely an illustration of our own experiences. Just remember: it will be inevitable that your veggies will catch a cold – the key is to learn how to overcome them to achieve a healthy crop come the following growing season.

## Deficiency

**Symptoms:** This begins with a paling on the leaf between the veins, eventually turning brown and dying due to poor soil fertility.

**Probable cause:** It usually occurs when the soil is tested and results are indicated at either end of the pH scale. This could mean low or depleted levels of N, P and K.

**Remedy:** Apply the appropriate liquid feed over the growing season to boost fruiting crops – such as a comfrey tea. Test the soil pH and rectify. It may be very acidic or far too limey. Add organic matter to improve the soil structure and aerate before planting next year's crop.

*Vine weevil*
*Keep an eye open for this little bug – the vine weevil, especially where plants are grown in containers or undercover, as it is one of the most common and devastating garden pests.*

## Squash Bugs

**Symptoms:** Leaves with pale green patches, which wilt and blacken.

**Probable cause:** Squash bugs. Adults are brownish-black and 1/2" long. Young bugs are whitish-green with dark heads and legs. Eggs are bright orange and laid on undersides of leaves.

**Remedy:** Handpick off adults and eggs. Trap the bugs before they reach the plant by laying a board near the affected plants. The bugs will find sanctuary underneath it and can be removed each morning.

## Potato Blight

**Symptoms:** A plague of black or brown blotches that appear on the potato leaves. This can affect your whole crop as well as your neighbour's within a matter of days. More severe cases will show as the plant turns yellow and eventually dies. As the illness seeps into the soil, the tubers (potatoes in the ground) will rot very quickly and any harvested will not store well.

**Remedy:** It can be treated by spraying the whole crop with a copper-based fungicide such as Bordeaux mixture, but it may be a pointless task if other less diligent plotholders are suffering with it. Otherwise, remove any of the affected leaves (this will slow the growth rate) and burn. Alternatively, cut back the whole plant to ground level – this should save the crop, although there will be a smaller harvest. Look out for blight-resistant varieties when choosing seed potatoes for the next season.

## Rust

**Symptoms:** A fungal disease of certain types of vegetables (in our case mainly leeks) that results in reddish or brownish patches of powdery spots on the leaves – it looks just like rust. Rust infections usually don't kill the affected vegetable but, with leeks usually planted close together, it can spread by the wind and rain over the entire crop. Luckily, it only affects the outer layers, which are peeled back and removed for cooking.

**Control:** No real solution to this problem in terms of treatment. Do not compost any diseased crop at the season's end, but burn. Test the soil pH to make sure it's not too Nitrogen-rich. Good hygiene – wash the dibber thoroughly before planting out next season's crop and give wider spacing for more air circulation between rows. Look out for rust-resistant varieties when choosing seed for the next season.

## Tomato Blight

**Symptoms:** As tomatoes are part of the same family as the potato, outdoor varieties suffer from exactly the same symptoms. This is a disease caused by a fungus-like organism, which spreads rapidly in the foliage. Black or brown blotches appear on the leaves in the early stages, which will then contaminate the fruits in wet weather, causing collapse and decay. (Plant outdoor varieties as far apart as space will allow from any potatoes you may have planted to try and limit the spread should either catch a cold.)

**Remedy:** Treat by spraying the whole crop with a copper-based fungicide such as Bordeaux mixture. Remove any diseased leaves as soon as noticed and burn. If it has spread, remove any fruits not affected – even the unripened green fruits can be turned into a chutney. Try growing in a greenhouse, which can offer protection from the weather.

## Cucumber Scab

**Symptoms:** Cucumber scab is caused by a fungus that can occur on leaves, the leafstalk and stems, but the most conspicuous symptoms occur on the fruit. Affected fruits are weakened and therefore often invaded by soft-rotting bacteria that produce a smelly decay.

## Scab Infection and Brown Rot

**Symptoms:** Blotches of olive-green or brown on the leaves of fruiting trees is known as scab. The blotches turn browner as time progresses and then appear on the fruit. The diseased leaves will fall early and the fruit will become increasingly covered. Eventually the fruit skin will crack, which in turn will allow brown rot into the fruit, spreading out from the wound caused by the infection. Brown rot will infect any wound on the fruit whether from scab, birds or other fruit-loving insect.

**Control:** Remove any diseased fruit and infected leaves as soon as noticed, then burn or compost. Prune out any infected spurs to reduce the fungus from spreading and infecting any healthy fruits still on the tree.

## Strawberry Fruit Rot

**Symptoms:** Berries usually spoil and get infection when touching the soil and remain damp after rain. Infection can start in any part of a berry that touches another decayed fruit or dead leaf and often results in grey mold, which spreads when the fruit is injured by frost or pests.

**Control:** The spacing of plants and the correct timing of fertiliser are the most important preventive measures. Disease is more severe when fertiliser is applied in the spring, or when rows are kept narrow. These practices result in lush foliage that prevents rapid drying of fruit after rain. Water on the foliage then results in suitable conditions for the development of rot.

Add straw under the foliage to raise the fruit off the ground and out of reach of wandering slugs with a free meal ticket.

**Diseases, Bugs, Pests**

## Slugs and Eggs

Slugs have both male and female organs, so every individual can lay up to 300 eggs each in batches of 10 to 50 with the potential to produce about 40,000 offspring. They hatch when the days start to warm above 5°C. Once hatched, they take less than a year to reach maturity and are usually nocturnal, but can be seen on dull damp days as well.

**Control:** Depending on how your garden grows, slug pellets, beer traps and nematodes are the first line of defence most gardeners will pitch for, otherwise a knitting needle and clothes pegs at dusk while on slug patrol can also be useful tools in the armoury. If gardening organically, try to encourage natural predators onto the plot, such as frogs and hedgehogs by leaving larger borders and growing wild flowers on your allotment.

## Cutworms

The equivalent of a lumberjack, this little pest cuts down your tender young seedling at the stem by eating it and felling the plant to be, hence the name cutworm. It's a moth caterpillar that lives in the upper layers of the soil and comes out at night to feast.

**Control:** As the cutworm will be buried under the soil, overwinter either as larvae or as pupae, the traditional autumn dig will kill many of the pests and expose many more to predators on the plot as a welcome treat.

## Carrot Fly

**Symptoms:** Carrot fly can smell your young tender carrots from the next county – laying eggs around the neck of the carrot, the newborn maggots tunnel and feast on the carrot flesh, causing the outsides to be marked with brown rings. This is often followed by rotting, which then encourages infestations of slugs.

**Control:** The first line of defence against this tiny pest is at the sowing stage. As the fly can only hover about 50cm above the ground, build a screen of fine mesh surrounding the crop or sow and cover with a micro-mesh tunnel. Alternatively, you could build raised beds above this height to ensure a healthy crop. Beer traps are also advisable to lure the slug population away from the young tender shoots.

## Centipedes

These are carnivores, so they eat the bad guys on the allotment that chew up your fruit and veg. So slugs and snails are on their menu. For the most part they are beneficial to the plot; however, as they are carnivorous, worms unfortunately are also fair game to them.

## Tomato Fruit Cracking

**Symptoms:** As pictured, cracking of the fruit is associated with wide fluctuations in water availability to the plant during the ripening stage. Prolonged dry spells in the weather followed by heavy rains and high temperatures may result in this symptom.

**Remedy:** Mulching and avoiding heavy applications of nitrogen fertiliser should help reduce fruit cracking. Growing tomatoes undercover where water and feed application are in a controlled environment should help overcome the problem.

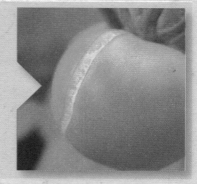

## Bolting or Flowering

**Symptoms:** This usually occurs in dry, hot weather when rainfall has been scarce for a number of weeks. The plant's reproduction system naturally activates producing an elongated stalk with flowers into which the plant focuses its energy. This condition occurs in vegetables that are grown mainly for their leaves: cabbage, lettuce, spinach, basil etc. Rhubarb is a prime example and will flower rapidly, when the weather permits, with an impressive display.

**Remedy:** This can be achieved by first watering and then applying a mulch to seal in the water around the base of the vegetable delaying or preventing the symptom. It may be beneficial to apply a feed such as pelleted chicken manure or a diluted comfrey tea. With regards to rhubarb, discard the flower as soon as it appears. When the crown has established itself (about five years), it can be divided into several sections with a spade, making sure each has a large bud – replant in a hole mixed with compost and manure. This is best done in the autumn.

## Caterpillars

Some are colourful, hairy and poisonous! Like the one pictured, the Cinnabar moth caterpillar, can be seen on ragwort, coltsfoot and groundsel happily chewing up the plant but of little threat to your crop – don't let children play with this variety. However, it is rarely seen.

Others are like marching soldiers: tiny green wormlike battalions of small and large white caterpillars, courtesy of the cabbage white butterflies happily flirting around your brassicas. Unless they are netted or covered over, expect the invasion. Look out for any eggs on the underside of the leaves, anything up to 100. Rub them off before they mature and start to nibble. Look out for the telltale signs and pick off any that have survived. **Check continuously!**

## Whitefly

This tiny white winged bug will be found in the hundreds. It's mainly on the underside of most brassica family veg (cabbage, brussels sprouts, cauliflower etc), damaging your crop by feeding on the sap. Give the plant a small shake and see if a white cloud radiates from the leaves.

**Control:** Net and cover your brassica veg as early in the season as possible to stop those pretty butterflies from laying eggs. Organic and chemical control is available on the market, but this bug is usually tolerated on the allotment – probably due to the relatively small amount of damage done.

## Weeds

They grow fast and in abundance, so it's a constant battle with the hoe over the summer months. There are two types of weed: annual and perennial, and both are a pain. Annuals are a nuisance because they grow fast and complete their life cycle within 12 months or before the first frosts come, by which time they could have released several thousand seeds for you to weed next season. Perennial weeds are also a big nuisance with long taproots, which are stubborn to dig out. Some root systems can cover several square feet, sending up shoots in-between your neat rows of veg.

**Control:** I have seen plotholders using chemical-based sprays to kill off weeds, but remember this rules out growing organically. Others use a strimmer to trim back fallow ground and paths, but for the most part it's traditionally hand-weeding for the best results.

## Furries

Crop damage from the local population of squirrels, rats, mice and rabbits is very difficult to contain and soul-destroying if you are ever unfortunate enough to suffer an attack.

Sweetcorn is their favoured crop, which you will have watched grow slow and steady over a number of months, when just about ripe for the picking – disaster. If you are a weekend gardener and the mice find your crop at the beginning of the week, come the following weekend's visit, the whole crop will have been raided and resigned to the compost bin. When building your defence, ensure it is strong and sturdy with no gaps in the barricade.

## Wood Pigeons

The allotment vandal! Wood pigeons have no respect for your hard-grown crops, be it fruit or veg, young and tender or mature fruit bushes. Unless protected, they will strip a currant bush bare and tear cabbage leaves to shreds, with only the fibrous skeletons left sticking up in the air – as illustrated.

**Control:** The only real defence is to cover young seedlings with netting: cabbage, cauliflower, brussels sprouts are all on the menu.

**FORGET CDs** as a cheap way of scaring pigeons. Trust me, they **DO NOT WORK!** Remember this to avoid disappointment. It is no surprise that wood pigeons are so fat!

## Ladybirds

Probably the most recognised of all insects, the ladybird beetle is no foe to the allotment fruit and veg grower as they will very happily eat all the aphids and whitefly on the plot.

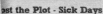

*Another one of the good guys. These things may look a bit strange on first impression, but they are most welcome to the vegetable grower. The ladybird larva is an efficient predator of the overwhelming aphid.*

Lost
the
Pl🍴t
PART

Magic Beans

# Magic Beans

Are you tickled pink with this year's achievements
or blushing red with the embarrassment of all those
letters received from the committee?

**Now is the time to start planning for next year's
success, and with a little forward-thinking, summer
self-sufficiency is sure to follow. Make a list of what
fruit and veg you would like to grow, and plan when
and where to sow them and the conditions they like.
Sketch out ideas or plans for those raised beds or
invest in that polytunnel to extend your growing season.**

Me, I got these in exchange for a cow, from an
old man I met on the way to the allotment.

Magic beans!

## Pickle, preserve, dry, store

A good allotment gardener knows how to extend the growing season and maximise return on all those hours invested. You are prepared not only for the growing season ahead on site, but also for the preparation in the kitchen. This is a key factor to your year-long veg self-sufficiency.

With the abundance of fresh summer fruit and veg shared with friends and family, you will still hopefully have tonnes left over. This is the opportunity for the home cook to shine. Pickled veg, fruit jams, chutney and sorbets all take time to prepare: gathering recipes, sterilising jars and getting all the ingredients ready. Equally, as much thought can go *into* the 'pot' as it does *on* the 'plot'.

We have been caught out with our first season's yield as inexperienced plotholders and our own ill-prepared kitchen, after having sown out almost every seed in each packet as illustrated earlier in the book. The lesson learnt is to plan ahead how to store and preserve your harvest if it's not direct from plot to pot.

Remember, the fruits of your labour do have a monetary value as does all fresh produce, and after all your initial investment, it's a worthwhile profit. So plan for the harvest festival, otherwise it's all compost!

**This is an idea of just what can be done to ensure a continuous veg supply over the less productive winter months.**

- potatoes when lifted can be left out for the soil to dry then stored in breathable hessian sacks in a dark cool shed or pantry
- chillies can be air-dried in the sun – threaded with needle and cord or made into oils
- onions and garlic can be strung and hung in the traditional fashion
- beans can be shelled and stored in jars
- garden peas can be frozen
- pumpkins and squashes, shelved in the dry
- tomatoes, made into soups and sauces, can be frozen in meal-size portions
- apples, wrapped in paper and stored in trays
- cucumbers and gherkins, pickled in jars
- carrots can even be layered in sand

If you are really struggling for space, it may be worthwhile looking at the traditional 'clamp'. I have never used this method myself, but it may be an option you wish to explore. Basically, it's a layered straw mound of root veg, which is covered and compacted with earth to make it watertight – squirreled away on the plot.

Home-made pickles, jams and chilli oils make wonderful Christmas presents too – showing that personal touch. Just another idea to inspire you when it comes to all your gluts of summer fruit and veg.

1. A crop of chillies in a glass tumbler drying on the kitchen windowsill.
2. Glass jars collected in anticipation of the bumper harvest to come.
3. Collect plastic containers for sorbets, soups and sauces.
4. Beans shelled for drying and storing.

**1**

**2**

**3**

**4**

## Vegetable and soil management

Four growing areas, plots or raised beds in the garden named **A**, **B**, **C** and **D** colour-coded for quick reference.

# Key: Crop Cycle

|  | Plot: A | Plot: B | Plot: C | Plot: D |
|---|---|---|---|---|
| **Season: 1** | ● | ■ | ▲ | ✖ |
| **Season: 2** | ✖ | ● | ■ | ▲ |
| **Season: 3** | ▲ | ✖ | ● | ■ |
| **Season: 4** | ■ | ▲ | ✖ | ● |

Diagram indicates the cycle of the potato ● over the 4 year (season) rotation around the allotment (plots: A – D).

# Key: Crop Order

This is the order of crops sown or planted in bed 'A' over a 4-year cycle:

Manure is added to the bed first: **Yr 1** = Potatoes, **Yr 2** = Peas. Add lime: **Yr 3** = Cabbage, **Yr 4** = Onions. Start over again.

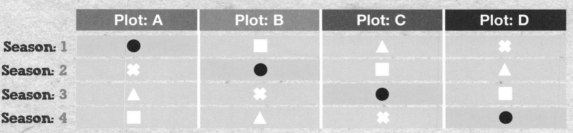

## + Add manure or compost

| | | |
|---|---|---|
| **Season: 1** | ● | Potatoes and tomatoes |
| **Season: 2** | ✖ | Peas and beans. Root veg: parsnips, carrots etc |

## + Add lime if necessary

| | | |
|---|---|---|
| **Season: 3** | ▲ | Cabbage, sprouts, broccoli etc |
| **Season: 4** | ■ | Onion, shallots, leeks, garlic, lettuce, sweetcorn etc |

These diagrams aim to explain the process of rotating your veg around the plot so as not to incubate pests and disease in the soil.

They also indicate which groups of veg follow on from the previous growing season and when to add manure and lime to balance your soil pH to suit the fruit and vegetables you intend to grow.

## Crop Rotation

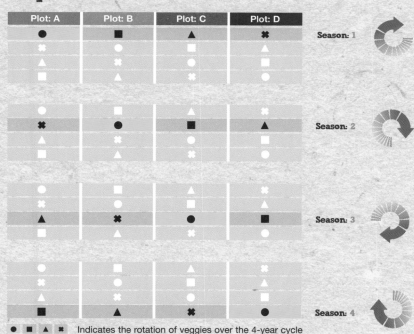

● ■ ▲ ✖  Indicates the rotation of veggies over the 4-year cycle

**Crop rotation is very simple.** Depending on the size of your plot or kitchen garden you can work it into a 3, 4 or 5-year cycle; the longer the better. The golden rule is not to plant, sow or grow a vegetable from the same family into the same place in the following year(s).

This concept can be applied to the rotation of manure. This tends to be introduced as it follows the crop order around the garden, which is then followed by the application of lime. This is to balance the soil pH (acidity or alkalinity on which 7 is neutral. Lower values are more acid and higher values more alkaline). Potatoes love manure-rich soil so this is a good starting point for your crop order.

## Manure Rotation

| Plot: A | | | | Plot: B | | | | Plot: C | | | | Plot: D | | | |
|---|---|---|---|---|---|---|---|---|---|---|---|---|---|---|---|
| A | W | S | **S** | A | W | S | S | A | W | S | S | A | W | S | S |
| A | W | S | S | **A** | **W** | **S** | S | A | W | S | S | A | W | S | S |
| A | W | S | S | A | W | S | S | A | W | S | **S** | A | W | S | S |
| A | W | S | S | A | W | S | S | A | W | S | S | A | **W** | S | **S** |

**S** Spring: Add manure

## Lime Rotation

| | Plot: A | | | | Plot: B | | | | Plot: C | | | | Plot: D | | | |
|---|---|---|---|---|---|---|---|---|---|---|---|---|---|---|---|---|
| Year: 1 | A | W | S | S | A | W | S | S | ▲ | W | ▲ | S | A | W | S | S |
| **Year: 2** | A | W | S | S | A | W | S | S | A | W | S | S | ▲ | W | ▲ | S |
| Year: 3 | ▲ | W | ▲ | S | A | W | S | S | A | W | S | S | A | W | S | S |
| **Year: 4** | A | W | S | S | ▲ | W | ▲ | S | A | W | S | S | A | W | S | S |

▲ Winter/summer brassicas: test soil – add lime if necessary

Rotation example: **Plot: B**, add manure in the spring of **Year 2**.
Rotation example: **Plot: B**, test soil pH – add lime if required in **Year 4**.

# Sowing Season: Brassicas (Cabbages)

## Brussels Sprouts
Sow undercover · Plant out · Sow outdoors · Harvest
J F M A M J J A S O N D

## Cabbage: Spring
Sow undercover · Plant out · Sow outdoors · Harvest
J F M A M J J A S O N D

## Cabbage: Summer
Sow undercover · Plant out · Sow outdoors · Harvest
J F M A M J J A S O N D

## Cabbage: Autumn
Sow undercover · Plant out · Sow outdoors · Harvest
J F M A M J J A S O N D

## Cabbage: Winter
Sow undercover · Plant out · Sow outdoors · Harvest
J F M A M J J A S O N D

## Cabbage: Savoy
Sow undercover · Plant out · Sow outdoors · Harvest
J F M A M J J A S O N D

## Calabrese
Sow undercover · Plant out · Sow outdoors · Harvest
J F M A M J J A S O N D

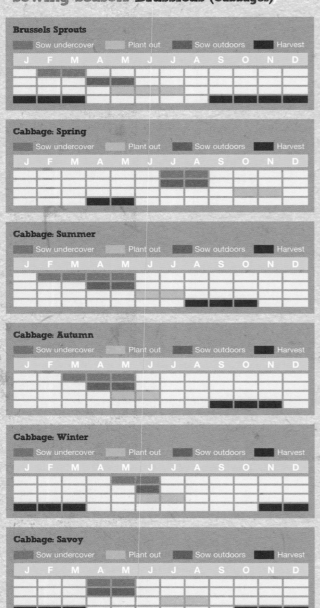

## Cauliflower: Early Summer
Sow undercover · Plant out · Sow outdoors · Harvest
J F M A M J J A S O N D

## Cauliflower: Summer/Autumn
Sow undercover · Plant out · Sow outdoors · Harvest
J F M A M J J A S O N D

## Cauliflower: Winter/Spring
Sow undercover · Plant out · Sow outdoors · Harvest
J F M A M J J A S O N D

## Kale
Sow undercover · Plant out · Sow outdoors · Harvest
J F M A M J J A S O N D

## Sprouting Broccoli
Sow undercover · Plant out · Sow outdoors · Harvest
J F M A M J J A S O N D

**Know your onions:** They can be sown and grown from seed, nurtured into young seedlings, and sown out when about the thickness of a pencil – just like leeks. However, with sets and thanks to the seed suppliers, most of the hard work is done for you. Supplied in a state of hibernation, these sets just need planting in neat straight rows either in autumn or late spring. **Red, white or yellow – the choice is yours.**

Knowing your onions means 'to be experienced in or knowledgeable about a subject'.

If you're still excited about growing your own by the end of your first season on the plot, you'll be a year wiser and well on your way to knowing your onions.

## Sowing Season: **Legumes** (Peas, Beans)

## Sowing Season: **Alliums** (Onion Family)

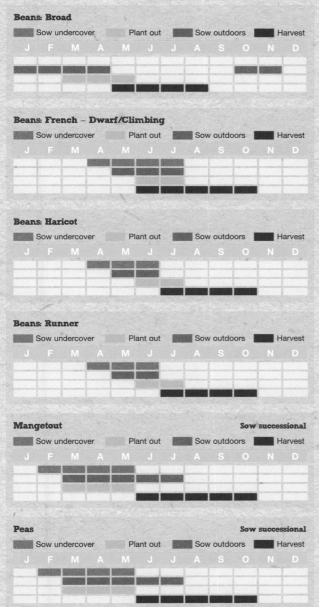

**Beans: Broad** — Sow undercover | Plant out | Sow outdoors | Harvest — J F M A M J J A S O N D

**Beans: French – Dwarf/Climbing** — Sow undercover | Plant out | Sow outdoors | Harvest — J F M A M J J A S O N D

**Beans: Haricot** — Sow undercover | Plant out | Sow outdoors | Harvest — J F M A M J J A S O N D

**Beans: Runner** — Sow undercover | Plant out | Sow outdoors | Harvest — J F M A M J J A S O N D

**Mangetout** — Sow successional — Sow undercover | Plant out | Sow outdoors | Harvest — J F M A M J J A S O N D

**Peas** — Sow successional — Sow undercover | Plant out | Sow outdoors | Harvest — J F M A M J J A S O N D

**Garlic** — Sow undercover | Plant out | Sow outdoors | Harvest — J F M A M J J A S O N D

**Leeks** — Sow undercover | Plant out | Sow outdoors | Harvest — J F M A M J J A S O N D

**Onions: Seed** — Sow undercover | Plant out | Sow outdoors | Harvest — J F M A M J J A S O N D

**Onions: Sets** — Sow undercover | Plant out | Sow outdoors | Harvest — J F M A M J J A S O N D

**Shallots** — Sow undercover | Plant out | Sow outdoors | Harvest — J F M A M J J A S O N D

**Spring Onions** — Sow undercover | Plant out | Sow outdoors | Harvest — J F M A M J J A S O N D

## Growing Season: **Fruit trees, bushes and plants**

If you are able to plant fruiting bushes and trees on your plot in the first season, then autumn is the best time of year for this. Early spring, as soon as the ground has thawed out and is warm enough, is also a good time. Remember, fruiting plants and trees need a few growing seasons to establish a good root system before they will put on a really good display of fruit. Depending on the varieties you have chosen they may need supports erecting and frames constructed – so a little research is advisable. **Note:** When buying fruit trees look out for the 'root stock' and whether they are of the self-fertile variety or need a pollinator tree for company.

## Beetroots — Sow successively

Legend: ▓ Sow undercover ░ Plant out ▬ Sow outdoors ■ Harvest

| J | F | M | A | M | J | J | A | S | O | N | D |
|---|---|---|---|---|---|---|---|---|---|---|---|
|  |  |  |  |  |  |  |  |  |  |  |  |
|  | ▬ | ▬ | ▬ | ▬ | ▬ | ▬ |  |  |  |  |  |
|  |  |  |  |  | ■ | ■ | ■ | ■ | ■ |  |  |

## Carrots: Early — Sow successively

Legend: ▓ Sow undercover ░ Plant out ▬ Sow outdoors ■ Harvest

| J | F | M | A | M | J | J | A | S | O | N | D |
|---|---|---|---|---|---|---|---|---|---|---|---|
|  |  |  |  |  |  |  |  |  |  |  |  |
|  |  | ▬ | ▬ | ▬ |  |  |  |  |  |  |  |
| ■ | ■ | ■ |  |  |  |  |  |  |  |  |  |

## Carrots: Main Crop — Sow successively

Legend: ▓ Sow undercover ░ Plant out ▬ Sow outdoors ■ Harvest

| J | F | M | A | M | J | J | A | S | O | N | D |
|---|---|---|---|---|---|---|---|---|---|---|---|
| ▓ | ▓ | ▓ |  |  |  |  |  |  |  |  |  |
|  |  |  |  |  |  |  |  |  |  |  |  |
|  |  |  |  |  | ■ | ■ | ■ | ■ | ■ | ■ |  |

## Celeriac

Legend: ▓ Sow undercover ░ Plant out ▬ Sow outdoors ■ Harvest

| J | F | M | A | M | J | J | A | S | O | N | D |
|---|---|---|---|---|---|---|---|---|---|---|---|
|  |  | ▓ | ▓ |  |  |  |  |  |  |  |  |
|  |  |  |  |  |  |  |  |  |  |  |  |
| ■ | ■ | ■ | ■ |  |  |  | ■ | ■ | ■ | ■ | ■ |

## Celery – Self-blanching

Legend: ▓ Sow undercover ░ Plant out ▬ Sow outdoors ■ Harvest

| J | F | M | A | M | J | J | A | S | O | N | D |
|---|---|---|---|---|---|---|---|---|---|---|---|
|  |  | ▓ | ▓ |  |  |  |  |  |  |  |  |
|  |  |  |  | ░ |  |  |  |  |  |  |  |
|  |  |  |  |  |  | ■ | ■ | ■ |  |  |  |

## Florence Fennel

Legend: ▓ Sow undercover ░ Plant out ▬ Sow outdoors ■ Harvest

| J | F | M | A | M | J | J | A | S | O | N | D |
|---|---|---|---|---|---|---|---|---|---|---|---|
|  |  | ▓ | ▓ |  |  |  |  |  |  |  |  |
|  |  |  | ▬ | ▬ |  |  |  |  |  |  |  |
|  |  |  |  | ■ | ■ | ■ | ■ | ■ |  |  |  |

## Parsnips

Legend: ▓ Sow undercover ░ Plant out ▬ Sow outdoors ■ Harvest

| J | F | M | A | M | J | J | A | S | O | N | D |
|---|---|---|---|---|---|---|---|---|---|---|---|
|  |  | ▬ | ▬ |  |  |  |  |  |  |  |  |
|  |  |  |  |  |  |  |  |  |  |  |  |
| ■ | ■ | ■ |  |  |  |  |  | ■ | ■ | ■ | ■ |

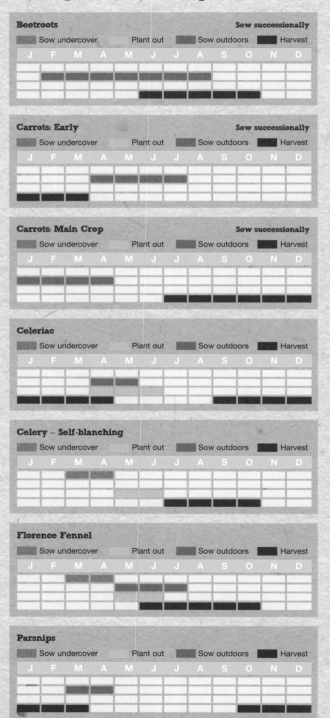

## Swedes

Legend: ▓ Sow undercover ░ Plant out ▬ Sow outdoors ■ Harvest

| J | F | M | A | M | J | J | A | S | O | N | D |
|---|---|---|---|---|---|---|---|---|---|---|---|
|  |  |  |  |  |  |  |  |  |  |  |  |
|  |  |  |  | ▬ | ▬ |  |  |  |  |  |  |
|  |  |  |  |  |  |  |  |  | ■ | ■ | ■ |

## Turnips

Legend: ▓ Sow undercover ░ Plant out ▬ Sow outdoors ■ Harvest

| J | F | M | A | M | J | J | A | S | O | N | D |
|---|---|---|---|---|---|---|---|---|---|---|---|
|  |  |  | ▬ | ▬ | ▬ | ▬ |  |  |  |  |  |
|  |  |  |  |  |  |  |  |  |  |  |  |
|  |  |  |  | ■ | ■ | ■ | ■ |  |  |  |  |

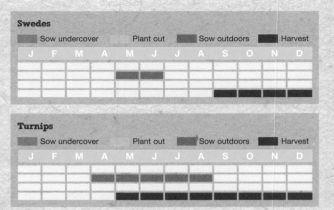

Growing your own veg is easy. If you get the bug, it's pretty good fun too. Just get the basics right in the first few months and the seeds will do the rest with a little help.

They're so eager that some will even try to grow in the fridge...

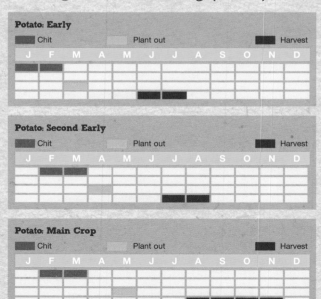

# Sowing Season: Root Veg (Potato)

## Potato: Early

Legend: ▬ Chit ░ Plant out ■ Harvest

| J | F | M | A | M | J | J | A | S | O | N | D |
|---|---|---|---|---|---|---|---|---|---|---|---|
| ▬ | ▬ |  |  |  |  |  |  |  |  |  |  |
|  |  |  |  |  |  |  |  |  |  |  |  |
|  |  |  |  |  | ■ | ■ |  |  |  |  |  |

## Potato: Second Early

Legend: ▬ Chit ░ Plant out ■ Harvest

| J | F | M | A | M | J | J | A | S | O | N | D |
|---|---|---|---|---|---|---|---|---|---|---|---|
|  | ▬ | ▬ |  |  |  |  |  |  |  |  |  |
|  |  |  |  | ░ |  |  |  |  |  |  |  |
|  |  |  |  |  | ■ | ■ |  |  |  |  |  |

## Potato: Main Crop

Legend: ▬ Chit ░ Plant out ■ Harvest

| J | F | M | A | M | J | J | A | S | O | N | D |
|---|---|---|---|---|---|---|---|---|---|---|---|
|  | ▬ | ▬ |  |  |  |  |  |  |  |  |  |
|  |  |  |  |  |  |  |  |  |  |  |  |
|  |  |  |  |  |  |  |  | ■ | ■ | ■ | ■ |

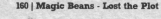

## Sowing Season: Salads

### Cucumbers
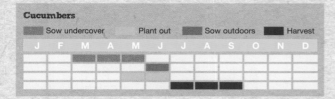

Sow undercover | Plant out | Sow outdoors | Harvest
J F M A M J J A S O N D

### Chicory
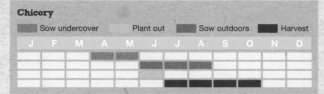

Sow undercover | Plant out | Sow outdoors | Harvest
J F M A M J J A S O N D

### Lettuce
Sow successionally
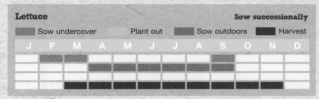

Sow undercover | Plant out | Sow outdoors | Harvest
J F M A M J J A S O N D

### Radish
Sow successionally
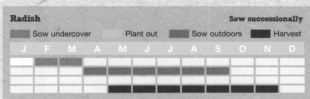

Sow undercover | Plant out | Sow outdoors | Harvest
J F M A M J J A S O N D

### Rocket
Sow successionally

Sow undercover | Plant out | Sow outdoors | Harvest
J F M A M J J A S O N D

### Tomato: Greenhouse
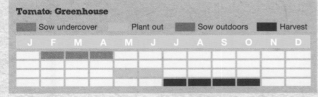

Sow undercover | Plant out | Sow outdoors | Harvest
J F M A M J J A S O N D

### Tomato: Outdoors
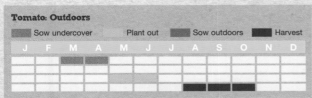

Sow undercover | Plant out | Sow outdoors | Harvest
J F M A M J J A S O N D

## Sowing Season: Tender Veg

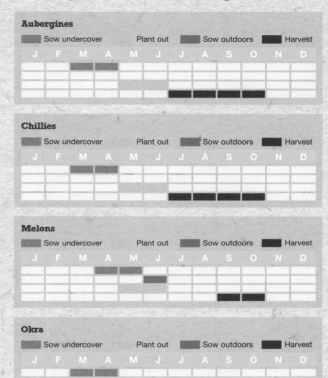

### Aubergines
Sow undercover | Plant out | Sow outdoors | Harvest
J F M A M J J A S O N D

### Chillies
Sow undercover | Plant out | Sow outdoors | Harvest
J F M A M J J A S O N D

### Melons
Sow undercover | Plant out | Sow outdoors | Harvest
J F M A M J J A S O N D

### Okra
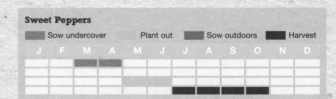

Sow undercover | Plant out | Sow outdoors | Harvest
J F M A M J J A S O N D

### Sweet Peppers
Sow undercover | Plant out | Sow outdoors | Harvest
J F M A M J J A S O N D

## Sowing Season: Successional

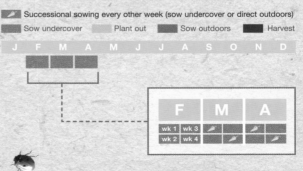

Successional sowing every other week (sow undercover or direct outdoors)

Sow undercover | Plant out | Sow outdoors | Harvest

J F M A M J J A S O N D

| | F | M | A |
|---|---|---|---|
| wk 1 | wk 3 | | |
| wk 2 | wk 4 | | |

# Herbs Belfast sink (back door) garden

Start off your herb garden as soon as the weather is warm enough. Buy a selection of your favourite herbs from the local garden centre or supermarket and harden off. Place some gravel or broken pots for drainage into the bottom of your sink or large pot and fill with a good-quality compost before planting. **Fresh herbs all summer long**!

## Sowing Season: Squashes

**Courgettes**

Sow undercover ▪ Plant out ▪ Sow outdoors ▪ Harvest

| J | F | M | A | M | J | J | A | S | O | N | D |
|---|---|---|---|---|---|---|---|---|---|---|---|

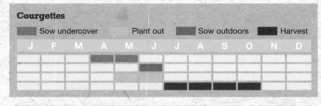

**Marrows**

Sow undercover ▪ Plant out ▪ Sow outdoors ▪ Harvest

| J | F | M | A | M | J | J | A | S | O | N | D |
|---|---|---|---|---|---|---|---|---|---|---|---|

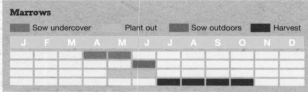

**Pumpkins**

Sow undercover ▪ Plant out ▪ Sow outdoors ▪ Harvest

| J | F | M | A | M | J | J | A | S | O | N | D |
|---|---|---|---|---|---|---|---|---|---|---|---|

**Squashes: Summer**

Sow undercover ▪ Plant out ▪ Sow outdoors ▪ Harvest

| J | F | M | A | M | J | J | A | S | O | N | D |
|---|---|---|---|---|---|---|---|---|---|---|---|

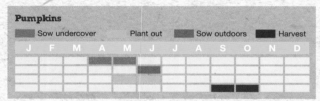

**Squashes: Winter**

Sow undercover ▪ Plant out ▪ Sow outdoors ▪ Harvest

| J | F | M | A | M | J | J | A | S | O | N | D |
|---|---|---|---|---|---|---|---|---|---|---|---|

**Sweetcorn**

Sow undercover ▪ Plant out ▪ Sow outdoors ▪ Harvest

| J | F | M | A | M | J | J | A | S | O | N | D |
|---|---|---|---|---|---|---|---|---|---|---|---|

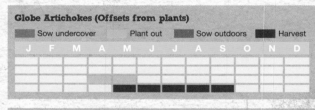

You could grow herbs down the allotment (and start them from seed), but we find it best to have them close to hand just for ease and picked fresh for cooking or cocktails.

## Sowing Season: Permanent Crops

**Asparagus (Crowns)**

Sow undercover ▪ Plant out ▪ Sow outdoors ▪ Harvest

| J | F | M | A | M | J | J | A | S | O | N | D |
|---|---|---|---|---|---|---|---|---|---|---|---|

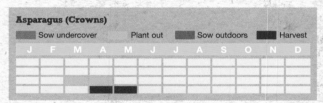

**Globe Artichokes (Offsets from plants)**

Sow undercover ▪ Plant out ▪ Sow outdoors ▪ Harvest

| J | F | M | A | M | J | J | A | S | O | N | D |
|---|---|---|---|---|---|---|---|---|---|---|---|

**Jerusalem Artichokes (Tubers)**

Sow undercover ▪ Plant out ▪ Sow outdoors ▪ Harvest

| J | F | M | A | M | J | J | A | S | O | N | D |
|---|---|---|---|---|---|---|---|---|---|---|---|

**Rhubarb (Sets from rootstocks)**

Sow undercover ▪ Plant out ▪ Sow outdoors ▪ Harvest

| J | F | M | A | M | J | J | A | S | O | N | D |
|---|---|---|---|---|---|---|---|---|---|---|---|

## Beer trap
A device or receptacle to hold a cocktail or brew intoxicating to slugs – a lure to trap.

## Cloche
A small translucent cover for protecting or forcing outdoor plants.

## Coldframe
A four-sided frame made up from boards or bricks with a removable glass or plastic top. The frame is placed on the ground and is used to house, protect, and harden off seedlings and small plants without artificial heat.

## Crop rotation
The action or system of rotating crops in order to keep the soil in good health.

## Double-dig
Digging two spits down into the soil. A method of soil cultivation where the soil is compacted and the ground has not been worked.

## F1/F2 hybrid
A vegetable made by combining two different elements; a mixture that results in a more tolerant or productive vegetable.

## Half plot
Description typically given to the size of a growing patch allocated to plotholders. Half the size of a full plot – which is now deemed too large for many newcomers to manage and due to current demand for space.

## Hardening-off
Inure a young plant to the cold by gradually increasing its exposure to it over a period of 7 – 14 days.

## Leaf mould
Soil consisting chiefly of decayed leaves, used as a growing medium in the nurturing of seed and young infant plants due to its qualities.

## Nematodes
A large phylum of worms with slender, unsegmented cylindrical bodies. They are found abundantly in soil and water and many are parasites that target slugs and snails.

## No-dig
A non-cultivation method used by some organic gardeners believed to promote a healthy soil community.

## N P K
Nitrogen (N), Phosphorus (P), Potassium (K)

## Nursery bed
An area of the plot used to raise young vegetables (usually planted close together) from which they are then planted out into their final growing position.

## Organic
Production of fruit and veg without the use of chemical fertilisers, pesticides, or any other artificial agents.

## Overwinter
An insect or plant living through the winter – able to survive cold temperatures.

## Perennials
Plants or weeds lasting or existing for a long or allegedly infinite amount of time.

## pH (Potential of Hydrogen)
A figure expressing the acidity or alkalinity of a solution on a logarithmic scale on which 7 is neutral. Lower values are more acid and higher values more alkaline.

## Raised bed
A method of growing contained within an area raised above ground level and filled with a material of choice.

## RHS
Royal Horticultural Society

## Ring culture
A method of growing greenhouse tomatoes that aids the development of roots, and partitions the feed and watering supplied to different levels in the root system.

## Shrub
A woody plant that is smaller than a tree and has several main stems arising at or near the ground.

## Spit
A layer of earth whose depth is equal to the length of the blade of a spade.

## Successional sowing
A term used to explain the method of sowing seed in small quantities over a set period of time.

## Trench-dig
Digging three or more spits down into the soil. A method of soil cultivation where the soil has poor drainage or large root systems from problem plants that need to be removed.

GLOSSARY

Lost the Plot

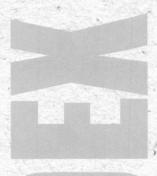

**Dedicated to Claire and Maya Sahara,** my girls, for their support and encouragement. Not only to take on an allotment in the first place, but for their understanding of how much family time has been dedicated to produce this book.

## Design:

**Paul King, Claire Lakey**
Design, layout, artwork, graphics, text and photography. www.twistedgifted.com

## Publishing and distribution:

**Allotment Junkie**
Social media, marketing and sales

## Editorial:

**Lorena Goldsmith**
Daniel Goldsmith Associates

**Proofreading**
Steve Jones

**Preview printing**
Print On – Cheadle

## Technical support and IT:

**Ian King**
Without your help none of this is possible

## Grow Your Own – expertise:

**National Society of Allotment and Leisure Gardeners Limited**
To all who took the time to read and review the book and for all the words of encouragement. www.nsalg.org.uk

**Association of Manchester Allotment Societies (AMAS)**
For your excitement and enthusiasm – which I found to be an inspiration. www.amas.org.uk

**Geoff Clark (Allotment Guru)**
For your encyclopaedic knowledge and generosity of time.

**Peter McCormick**
For your advice and wisdom from your years of passion for growing your own.

## From the allotment:

**Manchester City Council**
The landlord

**Southern Allotments Society**
To all on the committee for their dedication and commitment in running a family-friendly, safe environment, and for casting their experienced eyes over the content of this book.

**Kim, Kate, Karen and Patrick**
For being such lovely allotment neighbours.

**Mun Choong and Lydia**
For your kind words of encouragement as always.

**Roy**
Did I give you those books back?

## Family and friends:

**Ernest and Lorna (Mum and Dad)**
For the endless stream of reference materials, compost, pots and fruit bushes.

**Janet (Mum)**
I've named the pear tree you gave me – Janet.

**Tara and Mel**
Fruit trees for Christmas presents! Genius.

**Ian and Niki**
Thanks for the water butt guys.

**Chris, Nat and Grace**
Thanks for the handy DIY vouchers.

**Rachael, Jade and Rob**
For contributing to my reference library.

**Bryan and Chris**
Friendship and encouragement.

**Disclaimer**
We accept no responsibility for poor results due to acts of God, poor weather, drought, soil quality, out-of-date seeds, having a wheelbarrow flat tyre, magic beans, the allotment fairies or a lack of commitment on your part.

# Lost the Plot

## Next time

### Join us for the 'Main Course' – the next book in the series.

Following on from Part One, 'Extending the plot and the season – Part Two' is designed to take you to the next level. See what it takes to manage over 2000sq ft (a full plot), with even more ideas, advice and real-life photos of our successes and failures over the next two years as we become seasoned green thumbs.

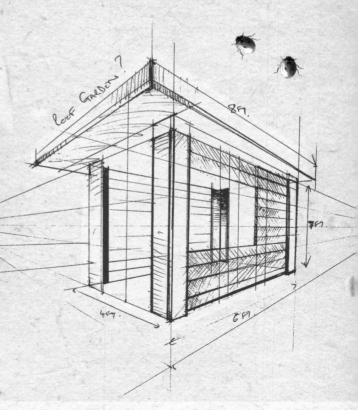

# Part Two:
## Extending the plot and the season

Taking on a full plot offers so much more in the way of opportunities for the kitchen gardener when it comes to your choice of what to sow and grow. The extra square footage means that an investment in a polytunnel is a real option and an aid to extending your growing season.

## Topics include:

- **Extending the plot**
- **Building compost bins**
- **Raising a polytunnel**
- **Putting up a shed**
- **Fruit support structures**

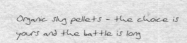

*Organic slug pellets - the choice is yours and the battle is long*

Eat your greens, Magic beans,
Pests and diseases, Crop rotation,
Sowing guide, Veg planner and
much, much more...

# MENU

## Welcome to our plot

### Lost the Plot

**Ingredients**
50% Perspiration, 50% Commitment

## Produced by
# a(l)otment JUNKIE

Continue with us into the next season and see how your family could benefit from growing your own in Part Two of the series. A little hard work and planning and you are rewarded with an abundance of crops throughout the year.

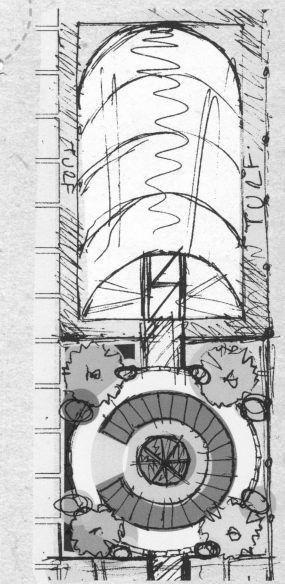

**Look at what's been cooking – the next book in the series:**

# www.allotmentjunkie.com

Join the Allotment Junkie community and interact with other growers:
www.facebook.com/allotmentjunkie    www.twitter.com/junkiesPlot